THE WORLD OF LATE ANTIQUITY

FROM MARCUS AURELIUS

TO MUHAMMAD

PETER BROWN

THAMES AND HUDSON · LONDON

1 FRONTISPIECE: a family group of the fourth century.
Gold glass inset in cross.

Picture research: Georgina Bruckner

© 1971 THAMES AND HUDSON LTD, LONDON

Printed and bound in Great Britain by Jarrold & Sons Ltd Norwich
ISBN 0 500 32022 5 CLOTHBOUND
ISBN 0 500 33022 0 PAPERBOUND

THE WORLD
OF LATE ANTIQUITY

John G. Howilson

CONTENTS

This book is a study of social and cultural change. I hope that the reader will put it down with some idea of how, and even of why, the Late Antique world (in the period from about AD 200 to about 700) came to differ from 'classical' civilization, and of how the headlong changes of this period, in turn, determined the varying evolution of western Europe, of eastern Europe and of the Near East.

To study such a period one must be constantly aware of the tension between change and continuity in the exceptionally ancient and well-rooted world round the Mediterranean. On the one hand, this is notoriously the time when certain ancient institutions, whose absence would have seemed quite unimaginable to a man of about AD 250, irrevocably disappeared. By 476, the Roman empire had vanished from western Europe; by 655, the Persian empire had vanished from the Near East. It is only too easy to write about the Late Antique world as if it were merely a melancholy tale of 'Decline and Fall': of the end of the Roman empire as viewed from the West; of the Persian, Sassanian empire, as viewed from Iran. On the other hand, we are increasingly aware of the astounding new beginnings associated with this period: we go to it to discover why Europe became Christian and why the Near East became Muslim; we have become extremely sensitive to the 'contemporary' quality of the new, abstract art of this age; the writings of men like Plotinus and Augustine surprise us, as we catch strains – as in some unaccustomed overture – of so much that a sensitive European has come to regard as most 'modern' and valuable in his own culture.

Looking at the Late Antique world, we are caught between the regretful contemplation of ancient ruins and the excited acclamation of new growth. What we often lack is a sense of what it was like to live in that world. Like many contemporaries of the changes we shall read about, we become either extreme conservatives or hysterical

7

2 An abstract art. The traditional consul's procession at Rome shown in the new idiom. From the fourth-century Basilica of Junius Bassus, Rome.

radicals. A Roman senator could write as if he still lived in the days of Augustus, and wake up, as many did at the end of the fifth century AD, to realize that there was no longer a Roman emperor in Italy. Again, a Christian bishop might welcome the disasters of the barbarian invasions, as if they had turned men irrevocably from earthly civilization to the Heavenly Jerusalem, yet he will do this in a Latin or a Greek unselfconsciously modelled on the ancient classics; and he will betray attitudes to the universe, prejudices and patterns of behaviour that mark him out as a man still firmly rooted in eight hundred years of Mediterranean life.

How to draw on a great past without smothering change. How to change without losing one's roots. Above all, what to do with the stranger in one's midst – with men excluded in a traditionally aristocratic society, with thoughts denied expression by a traditional culture, with needs not articulated in conventional religion, with the utter foreigner from across the frontier. These are the problems which every civilized society has had to face. They were particularly insistent in the Late Antique period. I do not imagine that a reader can be so untouched by the idea of classical Greece and Rome or so indifferent to the influence of Christianity, as not to wish to come to some judgment on the Late Antique world that saw the radical transformation of the one and the victory over classical paganism of the other. But I should make it plain that, in presenting the evidence, I have concentrated on the manner in which the men of the Late Antique world faced the problem of change.

The Roman empire covered a vast and diverse territory: the changes it experienced in this period were complex and various. They range from obvious and well-documented developments, such as the repercussions of war and high taxation on the society of the third and fourth centuries, to shifts as intimate and mysterious as those that affected men's relations to their own body and to their immediate neighbours. I trust that the reader will bear with me, therefore, if I begin the first part of this book with three chapters that sketch out the changes in the public life of the empire, from AD 200 to 400, and then retrace my steps to analyze those less public, but equally decisive, changes in religious attitudes that took place over the same period. I have done my best to indicate where I consider that changes in the social and economic conditions of the empire intermingled with the religious developments of the age.

Throughout this period, the Mediterranean and Mesopotamia are the main theatres of change. The world of the northern barbarians remained peripheral to these areas. Britain, northern Gaul, the Danubian provinces after the Slav invasions of the late sixth century fall outside my purview. The narrative itself gravitates towards the eastern Mediterranean; the account ends more naturally at the Baghdad of Harun al-Rashid than at the remote Aachen of his contemporary, Charlemagne. I trust that the reader (and especially the medievalist who is accustomed to surveys that concentrate on the emergence of a post-Roman western society) will forgive me if I keep to this area. For western Europe, he will have those sure guides, to whom we are both equally indebted.

No one can deny the close links between the social and the spiritual revolution of the Late Antique period. Yet, just because they are so intimate, such links cannot be reduced to a superficial relationship of 'cause and effect'. Often, the historian can only say that certain changes coincided in such a way that the one cannot be understood without reference to the other. A history of the Late Antique world that is all emperors and barbarians, soldiers, landlords and tax-collectors would give as colourless and as unreal a picture of the quality of the age, as would an account devoted only to the sheltered souls, to the monks, the mystics, and the awesome theologians of that time. I must leave it to the reader to decide whether my account helps him to understand why so many changes, of such different kinds, converged to produce that very distinctive period of European civilization – the Late Antique world.

The checking of this account owes much to the vigilance of Philip Rousseau, whose care reached, as usual, far beyond the castigation of dates and citations: its completion owes most to my wife, in whose curiosity and sensitivity to periods of change I have long been glad to share.

PART ONE: THE LATE ROMAN REVOLUTION

3 A baroque age. Daring arches and exuberant stone carving already betray a departure from the classical mood. The theatrical style provided a backdrop to communities that valued 'star' performers and magnificent public gestures. A typical local magnate made good, the emperor Septimius Severus (193–211), provided his home town, Lepcis Magna (Tunisia) with this and similar buildings.

I THE BOUNDARIES OF THE CLASSICAL WORLD: *c*. AD 200

'We live round a sea,' Socrates had told his Athenian friends, 'like frogs round a pond.' Seven hundred years later, in AD 200, the classical world remained clustered round its 'pond': it still clung to the shores of the Mediterranean. The centres of modern Europe lie far to the north and to the west of the world of ancient men. To travel to the Rhineland, for them, was to go 'half-way to the barbarians': one typical southerner even took his dead wife all the way back home, from Trier to Pavia, to bury her safely with her ancestors! A Greek senator from Asia Minor, posted to a governorship on the Danube, could only pity himself: 'The inhabitants . . . lead the most miserable existence of all mankind,' he wrote, 'for they cultivate no olives and they drink no wine.'

The Roman empire had been extended as far as had seemed necessary at the time of the republic and the early empire, to protect and enrich the classical world that had already existed for centuries round the coast of the Mediterranean. It is the extraordinary tide of Mediterranean life that strikes us about this empire at its apogee in the second century AD. This tide had washed further inland than ever previously; in North Africa and the Near East, it would never reach as far again. For a short time, an officers' mess modelled on an Italian country-villa faced the Grampians in Scotland. A chequer-board town, with amphitheatre, library and statues of classical philosophers looked out over the Hodna range, at Timgad, in what are now the bleak southern territories of Algeria. At Dura-Europos, on the Euphrates, a garrison-town observed the same calendar of public festivals as at Rome. The Late Antique world inherited this amazing legacy. One of the main problems of the period from 200 to 700 was how to maintain, throughout a vast empire, a style of life and a culture based originally on a slender coastline studded with classical city-states.

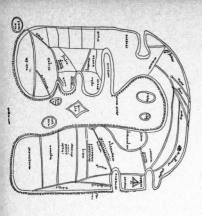

4 The frog pond. The eighth-century world map of Albi shows the Mediterranean as the centre of the world. Britain (top left) is a tiny shape; but the Nile Delta and the Euphrates (bottom centre and side) are shown in detail.

5 The sea means food. This fresco (between first and fourth centuries AD) from Ostia shows grain loaded on to a ship. According to a fifth-century observer, Constantinople was fortunate: 'Despite its vast population, food is always plentiful, because all kinds of provisions can be brought directly by sea from many regions.'

6 The alternative. Cumbersome travel by land. 'Our city,' wrote a fourth-century inhabitant of Asia Minor, 'being far from the sea, can neither get rid of its surplus nor import what it needs in times of shortage.' Relief from Adamklissi (Tropaeum Traiani), AD 108–109).

In the first place, the classical Mediterranean had always been a world on the edge of starvation. For the Mediterranean is a sea surrounded by mountain ranges: its fertile plains and river-valleys are like pieces of lace sewn on to sackcloth. Many of the greatest cities of classical times were placed within sight of forbidding highlands. Every year their inhabitants ransacked the surrounding countryside to feed themselves. Describing the symptoms of widespread mal-nutrition in the countryside in the middle of the second century, the doctor Galen observed: 'The city-dwellers, as was their practice, collected and stored enough corn for all the coming year immediately after the harvest. They carried off all the wheat, the barley, the beans and the lentils and left what remained to the countryfolk.' Seen in this light, the history of the Roman empire is the history of the ways in which 10 per cent of the population, who lived in the towns and have left their mark on the course of European civilization, fed themselves, in the summary manner described by Galen, from the labours of the remaining 90 per cent who worked the land.

Food was the most precious commodity in the ancient Mediter-ranean. Food involved transport. Very few of the great cities of the Roman empire could hope to supply their own needs from their immediate environment. Rome had long depended on the annual sailing of the grain-fleet from Africa: by the sixth century AD, Constantinople drew 175,200 tons of wheat a year from Egypt.

Water is to all primitive systems of transport what railways have been in modern times: the one, indispensable artery for heavy freight. Once a cargo left the waters of the Mediterranean or of a great river,

its brisk and inexpensive progress changed to a ruinous slow-motion. It cost less to bring a cargo of grain from one end of the Mediterranean to another than to carry it another seventy-five miles inland.

So the Roman empire always consisted of two, overlapping worlds. Up to AD 700, great towns by the sea remained close to each other: twenty days of clear sailing would take the traveller from one end of the Mediterranean, the core of the Roman world, to the other. Inland, however, Roman life had always tended to coagulate in little oases, like drops of water on a drying surface. The Romans are renowned for the roads that ran through their empire: but the roads passed through towns where the inhabitants gained all that they ate, and most of what they used, from within a radius of only thirty miles.

It was inland, therefore, that the heavy cost of empire was most obvious, along the verges of the great land routes. The Roman empire appears at its most cumbersome and brutal in the ceaseless effort it made to hold itself together. Soldiers, administrators, couriers, their supplies, had to be constantly on the move from province to province. Seen by the emperors in 200, the Roman world had become a cobweb of roads, marked by the staging-posts at which each little community would have to assemble ever-increasing levies of food, clothing, animals and manpower to support the court and the army.

As for those who served the needs of this rough machine, such compulsions were, at least, nothing new. In places, they were as old as civilization itself. In Palestine, for instance, Christ had warned his hearers how to behave when an official should 'requisition you to walk with him (carrying his baggage) for a mile'. Even the word the

13

Evangelist used for 'requisition' was not, originally, a Greek word: it derived from the Persian, it dated back over five hundred years, to the days when the Achaemenids had stocked the famous roads of their vast empire by the same rough methods.

Yet the Roman empire, that had sprawled so dangerously far from the Mediterranean by 200, was held together by the illusion that it was still a very small world. Seldom has a state been so dependent on so delicate a sleight of hand. By 200, the empire was ruled by an aristocracy of amazingly uniform culture, taste and language. In the West, the senatorial class had remained a tenacious and absorptive élite that dominated Italy, Africa, the Midi of France and the valleys of the Ebro and the Guadalquivir; in the East, all culture and all local power had remained concentrated in the hands of the proud oligarchies of the Greek cities. Throughout the Greek world no difference in vocabulary or pronunciation would betray the birthplace of any well-educated speaker. In the West, bilingual aristocrats passed unselfconsciously from Latin to Greek; an African landowner, for instance, found himself quite at home in a literary *salon* of well-to-do Greeks at Smyrna.

Such astonishing uniformity, however, was maintained by men who felt obscurely that their classical culture existed to exclude alternatives to their own world. Like many cosmopolitan aristocracies – like the dynasts of late feudal Europe or the aristocrats of the Austro-Hungarian empire – men of the same class and culture, in any part of the Roman world, found themselves far closer to each other than to the vast majority of their neighbours, the 'underdeveloped' peasantry on their doorstep. The existence of the 'barbarian' exerted a silent, unremitting pressure on the culture of the Roman empire. The 'barbarian' was not only the primitive warrior from across the frontier: by 200, this 'barbarian' had been joined by the non-participant within the empire itself. The aristocrat would pass from reassuringly similar forum to forum, speaking a uniform language, observing rites and codes of behaviour shared by all educated men; but his road stretched through the territories of tribesmen that were as alien to him as any German or Persian. In Gaul, the countrymen still spoke Celtic; in North Africa, Punic and Libyan; in Asia Minor, ancient dialects such as Lycaonian, Phrygian and Cappadocian; in Syria, Aramaic and Syriac.

Living cheek by jowl with this immense unabsorbed 'barbarian'

THE PROVINCIALS

7 (*below*) The rich Syrian. His long
Greek and Roman name – Marcus
Julius Maximus Aristides – is
accompanied by a long inscription in
Aramaic, and the sculptor has shown
him in the local style which anticipates
Byzantine portraits. Second–third
century AD.

8 (*right*) An Egyptian. Coptic
tombstone from Shech-Abade, Egypt,
fourth century AD.

9 Farmers from the Rhineland. The
short woollen tunic and hood of the
lower classes in the West continued
unchanged into medieval times, and
has survived as the monk's robe and
cowl. Second-century tombstone.

10 The protectors. Roman standard bearers from a local monument (the Tropaeum Traiani) at Adamklissi on the Danube frontier.

world, the governing classes of the Roman empire had kept largely free of some of the more virulent exclusiveness of modern colonial régimes: they were notoriously tolerant of race and of local religions. But the price they demanded for inclusion in their own world was conformity – the adoption of its style of life, of its traditions, of its education, and so of its two classical languages, Latin in the West and Greek in the East. Those who were in no position to participate were dismissed: they were frankly despised as 'country-bumpkins' and 'barbarians'. Those who could have participated and did not – most notably the Jews – were treated with varying degrees of hatred and contempt, only occasionally tempered by respectful curiosity for the representatives of an ancient Near Eastern civilization. Those who had once participated and had ostentatiously 'dropped out' – namely the Christians – were liable to summary execution. By AD 200 many provincial governors and many mobs had had occasion to assert the boundaries of the classical world with hysterical certainty against the

Christian dissenter in their midst: as one magistrate told Christians, 'I cannot bring myself so much as to listen to people who speak ill of the Roman way of religion.'

Classical society of about A D 200 was a society with firm boundaries. Yet it was far from being a stagnant society. In the Greek world, the classical tradition had already existed for some seven hundred years. Its first burst of creativity, at Athens, should not blind us to the astonishing way in which, from the time of the conquests of Alexander the Great, Greek culture had settled down to a rhythm of survival – as drawn-out, as capable of exquisite nuance, as patient of repetition as a plain-chant. One exciting renaissance had taken place in the second century A D. It coincided with a revival of the economic life and the political initiative of the upper classes of the Greek cities. The age of the Antonines was the heyday of the Greek Sophists. These men – known for their devotion to rhetoric – were at one and the same time literary lions and great urban nabobs. They enjoyed vast influence and popularity: one of them, Polemo of Smyrna, 'treated whole cities as his inferiors, emperors as not his superiors and gods . . . as equals'. Behind them stood the thriving cities of the Aegean. The huge classical remains at Ephesus and Smyrna (and, indeed, similar contemporary cities and temples, from Lepcis Magna in Tunisia to Baalbek in the Lebanon) seem to us nowadays to sum up a timeless ancient world. They were, in fact, the creation of only a few generations of baroque magnificence, between Hadrian (117–138) and Septimius Severus (193–211).

It is just at the end of the second and the beginning of the third centuries, also, that the Greek culture was garnered which formed the ballast of the classical tradition throughout the Middle Ages. The encyclopaedias, the handbooks of medicine, natural science and astronomy, to which all cultivated men – Latins, Byzantines, Arabs – turned for the next fifteen hundred years, were compiled then. Literary tastes and political attitudes that continued, in the Greek world, until the end of the Middle Ages, were first formed in the age of the Antonines: Byzantine gentlemen of the fifteenth century were still using a recondite Attic Greek deployed by the Sophists of the age of Hadrian.

At this time the Greek world made the Roman empire its own. We can appreciate this identification with the Roman state and the subtle shifts of emphasis it entailed, by looking at a Greek from

Bithynia, who had joined the Roman governing class as a senator – Dio Cassius, who wrote his *Roman History* up to AD 229. No matter how enthusiastically Dio had absorbed the outlook of the Roman Senate, we are constantly reminded that the empire had come to Greeks accustomed to centuries of enlightened despotism. Dio knew that the Roman emperor was an autocrat. Common decency and a shared interest with the educated upper classes were the only checks on his behaviour – not the delicate clockwork of the constitution of Augustus. And Dio knew how fragile such restraints could be: he had been present at a meeting of the Senate when an astrologer had denounced certain 'bald-pated men' for conspiring against the emperor . . . instinctively his hand had shot up to feel the top of his head. But Dio accepted the strong rule of one man as long as it gave him an orderly world: only the emperor could suppress civil war; only he could police the faction-ridden Greek cities; only he could make Dio's class secure and respected. Byzantine scholars who turned to Dio, centuries later, to know about Roman history, found themselves hopelessly at sea in his account of the heroes of the Roman republic: but they were able to understand perfectly the strong and conscientious emperors of Dio's own age – already the Roman history of a Greek of the late second and early third century AD was *their* history.

A shift of the centre of gravity of the Roman empire towards the Greek cities of Asia Minor, a flowering of a Greek mandarinate – in these ways, the palmy days of the Antonines already point in the direction of Byzantium. But the men of the age of Dio Cassius still resolutely faced the other way: they were stalwart conservatives; their greatest successes had been expressed in a cultural reaction; for them, the boundaries of the classical world were still clear and rigid – Byzantium proper, a civilization that could build, on top of this ancient backward-looking tradition, such revolutionary novelties as the establishment of Christianity and the foundation of Constantinople as a 'New Rome', was inconceivable to a man like Dio. (He never, for instance, so much as mentions the existence of Christianity, although Christians had worried the authorities in his home-country for over 150 years.) Such a civilization could only emerge in the late Roman revolution of the third and fourth centuries AD.

★

11 The shadow of Persia. The Roman emperor, Valerian, is shown bowing as a vassal before Shapur I, portrayed as the successor of Darius and Xerxes establishing his right to the eastern provinces of the Roman empire. Rock relief at Bishapur, second half of third century AD.

The theme that will emerge throughout this book is the shifting and redefinition of the boundaries of the classical world after AD 200. This has little to do with the conventional problem of the 'Decline and Fall of the Roman Empire'. The 'Decline and Fall' affected only the political structure of the western provinces of the Roman empire: it left the cultural power-house of Late Antiquity – the eastern Mediterranean and the Near East – unscathed. Even in the barbarian states of western Europe, in the sixth and seventh centuries, the Roman empire, as it survived at Constantinople, was still regarded as the greatest civilized state in the world: and it was called by its ancient name, the *Respublica* (see pp. 134–35). The problem that urgently preoccupied men of Late Antiquity themselves was, rather, the painful modification of the ancient boundaries.

Geographically, the hold of the Mediterranean slackened. After 410 Britain was abandoned; after 480 Gaul came to be firmly ruled from the north. In the East, paradoxically, the rolling-back of the Mediterranean had happened earlier and more imperceptibly; but it proved decisive. Up to the first century AD, a veneer of Greek civilization still covered large areas of the Iranian plateau: a Greco-Buddhist art had flourished in Afghanistan, and the decrees of a Buddhist ruler have been found outside Kabul, translated into impeccable philosophical Greek. In 224, however, a family from Fars, the 'Deep South' of Iranian chauvinism, gained control of the Persian empire. The revived Persian empire of this, the Sassanian, dynasty quickly shook the Greek fancy-dress from its shoulders. An efficient and aggressive empire, whose ruling classes were notably unreceptive to western influence, now stood on the eastern frontiers of the Roman empire. In 252, 257 and again in 260, the great Shahanshah, the king of kings, Shapur I, showed what terrible damage his mailed horsemen could do: 'Valerian the Caesar came against us with seventy thousand men . . . and we fought a great battle against him, and we took Valerian the Caesar with our own hands. . . . And the provinces of Syria, Cilicia and Cappadocia we burnt with fire, we ravaged and conquered them, taking their peoples captive.'

The fear of repeating such an experience tilted the balance of the emperor's concern further from the Rhine and ever nearer to the Euphrates. What is more, the confrontation with Sassanian Persia breached the barriers of the classical world in the Near East: for it gave prominence to Mesopotamia, and so exposed the Roman world to constant influence from that area of immense, exotic creativity in art and religion (see especially pp. 164–65).

It is not always the conventional dates that are the most decisive. Everyone knows that the Goths sacked Rome in 410: but the lost western provinces of the empire remained a recognizably 'sub-Roman' civilization for centuries. By contrast, when the eastern provinces of the empire were lost to Islam after 640, these did not long remain 'sub-Byzantine' societies: they were rapidly 'orientalized'. For Islam itself was pulled far to the east of its original conquests by the vast mass of the conquered Persian empire. In the eighth century the Mediterranean seaboard came to be ruled from Baghdad; the Mediterranean became a backwater to men who were used to sailing from the Persian Gulf; and the court of Harun al-Rashid (788–809), with its heavy trappings of 'sub-Persian' culture, was a reminder that the irreversible victory of the Near East over the Greeks began slowly but surely with the revolt of Fars in AD 224.

As the Mediterranean receded, so a more ancient world came to light. Craftsmen in Britain returned to the art forms of the La Tène age. The serf of late Roman Gaul re-emerged with his Celtic name – the *vassus*. The arbiters of piety of the Roman world, the Coptic hermits of Egypt, revived the language of the Pharaohs (see p. 94); and the hymn-writers of Syria heaped on Christ appellations of Divine Kingship that reach back to Sumerian times. Round the Mediterranean itself, inner barriers collapsed. Another side of the Roman world, often long prepared in obscurity (see pp. 41–42), came to the top, like different-coloured loam turned by the plough. Three generations after Dio Cassius had ignored it, Christianity became the religion of the emperors (see pp. 86ff.). Small things sometimes betray changes more faithfully, because unconsciously. Near Rome, a sculptor's yard of the fourth century still turned out statues, impeccably dressed in the old Roman toga (with a socket for detachable portrait-heads!); but the aristocrats who commissioned such works would, in fact, wear a costume which betrayed prolonged exposure to the 'barbarians' of the non-Mediterranean world – a woollen shirt from the Danube, a cloak from northern Gaul, fastened at the shoulders by a filigree brooch from Germany, even guarding their health by 'Saxon' trousers. Deeper still, at the very core of the Mediterranean, the tradition of Greek philosophy had found a way of opening itself to a different religious mood (see pp. 72ff.).

Such changes as these are the main themes of the evolution of the Late Antique world. In the next two chapters we must consider the political and social setting of the revolution with which these changes began in the late third and fourth centuries.

Dio Cassius lay down his pen in 229 with no sense of foreboding. His grandson and great-grandson could have witnessed the accession of Diocletian in 284, and the conversion of Constantine to Christianity in 312. To take a better-known example: St Cyprian, bishop of Carthage, was martyred in 258. Cyprian's secretary, as a very old man, was able to tell an elder friend of St Jerome (born in about 342) what books the great bishop had preferred reading. We should not overlook such humble links between the generations. The pagan Roman empire of a Cyprian in the mid-third century may seem to us infinitely removed from the Christian 'late' Roman empire of a Jerome in the late fourth century. Yet the Roman empire was a vast, slow-moving society. The overwhelming proportion of its wealth lay in agriculture, and most of its population lived from subsistence farming. It was, therefore, well cushioned against the effects of two generations of political instability and barbarian invasion after 240.

After 240, the sprawling empire had to face barbarian invasion and political instability on a scale for which it was totally unprepared. The terms on which the Roman empire weathered the crisis of the years between 240 and 300 set the tone for the future development of Late Antique society.

The crisis laid bare the contrast between the ancient Mediterranean core of the empire and the more primitive and fragile world along its frontiers. Round the Mediterranean, war had become a remote eventuality. The outright dominance of the traditional aristocracy in the politics and cultural life of the empire depended on prolonged peace. Yet, to the north and along the eastern frontier facing the highlands of Armenia and Iran, it was plain that peace was a momentary lull in the laws of nature. The Roman empire was one of the very few great states in the ancient world – along with China – that had so much as attempted to create an oasis of peaceful civilian government among societies that had always lived by war. With the rise of Persia in 224, the formation of the Gothic confederacy in the Danube basin after 248, and the pullulation of war-bands along the Rhine after 260, the empire had to face war on every front.

It was plainly ill-equipped to do so. Between 245 and 270, every frontier collapsed. In 251 the emperor Decius was lost with his army, fighting the Goths in the marshes of the Dobrudja. In 260 Shapur I

12 Diocletian (284–305) and his colleagues in battle dress. Fellow officers in a military junta, they clasp shoulders as a gesture of solidarity. This simplified, military group was so medieval in tone that the individuals were long mistaken for Christian crusaders, and even worshipped as statues of Saint George! Porphyry sculpture, San Marco, Venice.

took the emperor Valerian prisoner with his army and captured Antioch. Barbarian longboats from the Rhine estuary and the Crimea anticipated the feats of the Vikings. They ravaged the coasts of Britain and Gaul, and raided the helpless cities of the Aegean. In 271, the emperor Aurelian had to surround Rome itself with a bleak military wall. Even the unity of the empire was threatened by local 'emergency' empires: Postumus ruled Gaul, Britain and Spain from 260 to 268; Zenobia of Palmyra controlled part of the eastern provinces from 267 to 270.

The Roman world split apart. Different groups and different provinces fared very differently. Along the frontiers, villas and cities were suddenly deserted; the armies threw up twenty-five emperors in forty-seven years, only one of whom died in his bed. Round the Mediterranean, however, a more resilient world stuck to its ways and hoped for the best. The mint of Alexandria conscientiously registered the faces of emperors who came and went a thousand miles to the north. In their great villas, Roman senators continued to patronize Greek philosophy (see p. 70), and sat for their portrait-busts in the baroque manner of the Antonines. In Rome, in Africa and in the eastern Mediterranean, the Christian bishops enjoyed a tranquillity and freedom of movement that contrasted ominously with the hard-pressed existence of their pagan rulers (see pp. 66 ff.). In the decades of crisis, many leading inhabitants of Mediterranean towns must have gone quietly about the routine duties of administration, as those of Oxyrhynchus did in Upper Egypt, hoping that the 'divine good fortune' of the emperor would soon put everything right.

The solid bedrock of civilian life held firm. But the crisis had one immediate result: never again would the Roman world be ruled by a charmed circle of unquestioning conservatives, as in the days of Marcus Aurelius.

For the Roman empire was saved by a military revolution. Seldom has a society set about cutting out the dead wood in its upper classes with such determination. The senatorial aristocracy was excluded from military commands in about 260. The aristocrats had to make way for professional soldiers who had risen from the ranks. These professionals recast the Roman army. The unwieldy legion was broken up into small detachments, to provide a more flexible defence in depth against barbarian raiders. The frontier detachments were backed by an impressive new striking-force, made up of heavy

13 The world of the frontiers. Roman
soldiers fighting on the Danube.
Relief from Adamklissi, AD 108–09.

cavalry – the emperors' 'companions', the *comitatus*. These changes doubled the size of the army, and more than doubled its cost. A force of about 600,000 men, it was the largest single group the ancient world had ever seen. To serve its needs, the emperors expanded the bureaucracy. By AD 300, civilians were complaining that, as a result of the reforms of the emperor Diocletian (284–305), 'there were more tax-collectors than taxpayers'. As we shall see in our next chapter, the pressure of increased taxation inexorably moulded the structure of Roman society in the fourth and fifth centuries.

The military revolution of the late third century was treated with uncomprehending hostility by the conservative civilians of the time; and it has, in consequence, received little better treatment from some modern classical scholars. Yet it was one of the finest achievements of Roman statecraft. With their New Model army, Gallienus check-mated the barbarians in Yugoslavia and northern Italy in 258 and 268; Claudius II pacified the Danube frontier in 269; Aurelian swept through the eastern provinces in 273; and Galerius crushed the Persian menace in 296.

25

The soldiers and officers of those Danubian provinces, who had seemed so raw to the Mediterranean aristocrats of a previous age, emerged as the heroes of the imperial recovery of the late third and early fourth centuries. As one of them said, 'Twenty-seven years I have been in the service: never been court-martialled for looting or brawling. I have been through seven wars. I have never lagged behind anyone, been second to none in the fight. The captain has never seen me waver.' The army was an artesian well of talent. By the end of the third century, its officers and administrators had ousted the traditional aristocracy from control of the empire. The great reforming emperor of the age, Diocletian, was the son of a freedman from Dalmatia; his nominee, Galerius (305–11) had herded cattle in the Carpathians; another of his colleagues, Constantius Chlorus (305–06), was an obscure country-gentleman from near Naissus (Niš). They were men whose rise to power was as spectacular and as well merited as was that of Napoleon's marshals. They, and their successors, chose servants of similar background. The son of a pork butcher, of a small-

14 Constantius Chlorus, the soldier father of Constantine. Gold medal from the Beaurains Treasure, Arras Museum.

15 The imperial recovery. Constantius Chlorus arrives in London in 296: 'He brings us back the eternal light of Rome.' In the western provinces, the safety of the towns depended on such arrivals of the emperor at the head of his crack regiments of heavy cavalry. Copy of gold medallion from Trier.

16 'The dollar of the Middle Ages': a gold *solidus* of Constantine (306–37). In deliberate contrast to the rugged Diocletian, Constantine is shown as a civilian hero – with raised eyes and classical profile. Mint of Nicomedia.

town notary, of a cloakroom attendant in the public baths, became the praetorian prefects on whom the prosperity and stability of the eastern parts of the empire depended under Constantine and Constantius II.

The reign of Constantine, especially the period from 324 to 337, saw the final establishment of a new 'aristocracy of service' at the top of Roman society. They were salaried officials and were paid in the new, stable gold coinage – the *solidus*. In the fourth century this gold coin, the 'dollar of the Middle Ages', enjoyed the vast purchasing power of the modern dollar, in a society still in the grip of a dizzy inflation. Their positions in the army and the bureaucracy gave the imperial servants vast opportunities for profiteering in foodstuffs. As a contemporary wrote: 'Constantine was the first to open the provinces to his friends; Constantius II gorged them down to the marrow.'

After the conversion of Constantine in 312. the emperors and the majority of their courtiers were Christians. The ease with which Christianity gained control of the upper classes of the Roman empire

27

17, 18, 19, 20 The new Roman. A fourth-century official from the Danubian provinces. His slaves bring him his trousers (18), his cloak with pin (19), his bejewelled military belt (20). Frescoes from a tomb at Silistra (Bulgaria).

in the fourth century was due to the revolution that had placed the imperial court at the centre of a society of 'new' men, who found it comparatively easy to abandon conservative beliefs in favour of the new faith of their masters.

The new upper classes brought with them reminders of their brisk military origins. All officials wore uniform; even the emperors had abandoned the toga to appear, on their statues, in battle-dress. This battle-dress was the brutally simple uniform of the Danubian frontier – a small round helmet, a cloak with a shoulder-pin of barbarian workmanship, and a heavy inlaid belt. The Latin slang of the provinces was irremovably lodged in their official vocabulary: a classical Roman should have called the new gold piece an *aureus*; nobody called it anything but a *solidus* – a 'solid bit'.

Thus a new element, drawn from far beyond the traditional aristocracies of the empire, had come to stay in the governing class. Yet the social fluidity that had forced such men to the top was neither indiscriminate, nor did it embrace all of Roman society. In the East, for instance, Constantinople was an isolated whirlpool of change, whose currents only gradually affected the traditional upper-class society of the provinces. A Greek rhetor, Libanius (314–93), had to

perform there, in 341/42, before Latin-speaking soldiers who attended his speeches 'as if I were doing a dumb-show', for they could not follow his classical Greek. But he would retire to find more congenial company in a provincial town such as Nicomedia. Here he could still find 'well-born men', 'lovers of the Muses'.

For, outside the bustling world of the court and the army, the slow-moving traditionalist elements in the Roman world had survived. The great landowners had continued to amass great estates, and the classical system of education had continued to turn out young men groomed in conservative ways. Like the opposed vaults of a single arch, the 'new' society of imperial servants came to rest against the more rooted and backward-looking society of the educated upper classes. The absorptive power and the creativity of these upper classes was astonishing. At the end of the fourth century, for instance, rich Romans, whose grandfathers had perpetrated the brutal novelties of the Arch of Constantine, were patronizing exquisite neo-classical ivory-work, and knew more of Latin literature than most of their predecessors.

The ancient classical education provided the bridgehead between the two worlds. This culture, studiously absorbed, formed a *trompe l'œil* against which the new man could merge. As one provincial governor confessed: 'I came from a poor father in the countryside: now, by my love of letters, I have come to lead the life of a gentleman.' Much of the classical culture of the fourth century was a 'success-culture': its most egregious product was a mere thirty-page 'briefing' – a *breviarium* – of Roman history for the new rulers of the empire.

Yet it is precisely the self-conscious effort of a more fluid upper class to regain its roots in the past and to achieve a firm basis of cohesion that accounts for some of the most refined and delightful products of the Late Antique world. The new senators patronized luxury goods of exquisite craftsmanship to emphasize their status and their solidarity. They celebrated their dynastic matches with silver bridal chests (such as the Esquiline Casket in the British Museum); they announced the occasion to their friends in pure, neo-classical ivory tablets (such as the 'Nicomachi' diptych in the Victoria and Albert Museum). On such diptychs, they celebrated their holding of the consulship, in an elaborate heraldry that stressed the glory and antiquity of the title, rather than the new-won merits of its holder. But the most polished and traditional artefacts that passed between these men were, of course, their letters. These were as accomplished and as jejune as the visiting-cards of the mandarins of imperial China. The fourth and fifth centuries are the age of vast collections of letters, most of which were no more than the exquisite counters with which the governing class of the Roman world registered the very real losses and gains of a continuous struggle for privilege and influence.

The new governing classes needed scholars, and, in turn, the scholars came to staff the bureaucracy, and at moments dominated the court. Ausonius (*c.* 310–*c.* 395), a poet from Bordeaux, became an *éminence grise* of the western empire. It was possible for Augustine, a young man from a poor family in Thagaste (South Ahras) in Africa, to become professor of rhetoric at Milan at the age of thirty (in 384), and to consider a provincial governorship and an alliance with the local nobility as the next step in his career. In the Greek parts of the empire, the fusion of traditional scholar and new bureaucrat proved decisive. Men who shared such a uniform and backward-looking culture were the only stable focus in a bureaucratic machine that absorbed talent like a sponge. A constant influx of provincials needing

21 The classical renaissance. This ivory celebrated the marriage of a daughter of Symmachus (see p. 116), a pagan Roman senator of the late fourth century.

22 Wedding of a fourth-century aristocrat. The couple may have been Christian, but the occasion was frankly, and delightfully, pagan. Detail of the lid from the Bridal Casket of Secunda and Projectus.

to be carefully groomed in classical Greek literature in Constantinople gave the Byzantine governing class the illusory stillness of the surface of a mill-race. They provided the permanent civil servants and the provincial governors. It was they who would write the history of Byzantium for the next thousand years. So uniform was their culture that their last representative was still writing, under the Ottoman sultans in the late fifteenth century, a history of his own times in the manner of Thucydides.

Two features of this new upper class are worth emphasizing. First, alongside much blatant careerism, there was a genuine striving to create an élite. The classical culture of Late Antiquity was like a high-pitched pyramid: it strained at an 'aristocratization', at producing men 'raised by habitual discipline above the common mass of mankind'. Men sought, by studiously absorbing classical standards of literature and by modelling their behaviour on the ancient heroes, a stability, a certainty which they could no longer find in unself-conscious participation in a traditional way of life. They were men who were painfully aware that many of their roses were grafted on to a very primitive root stock. Only a meticulous dedication to the perfection of the ancients could save men, thus cast loose from traditional sanctions, from themselves. Julian the Apostate (361–63) genuinely believed that his brother Gallus had 'gone savage', but that he himself had been 'saved' by the gods, who had provided him with a university education. It is not surprising, therefore, that pagans and Christians fought so virulently throughout the fourth century as to whether literature or Christianity was the true *paideia*, the true Education: for both sides expected to be saved by education. The man who had chiselled and polished himself like a statue through devotion to the ancient classics was the highest ideal. He is shown on his sarcophagus, gazing quietly at an open book – a 'man of the Muses', a saint of classical culture. Soon he will become a saint: the Christian bishop with his open Bible, the inspired Evangelist crouched over his page, are direct descendants of the Late Antique portrait of the man of letters.

Secondly, no matter how high the pyramid might be pitched, it was always open at the base. Throughout the fourth century the teaching profession was an area of exceptional fluidity. Thus the ideal of classical culture was constantly fed by the enthusiasm of newcomers. The revolutionary 'conversion' of Constantine to Chris-

23 The man of culture – sitting in his teacher's chair (prototype of the bishop's *cathedra*), with a cupboard full of ancient scrolls of the classics. Roman relief.

24 Man of culture to evangelist. St Matthew from the *Gospels of Charlemagne*, Aachen, before AD 800.

tianity was not the only conversion in that age of change: there were many more silent but equally fanatical conversions to the traditional culture and to the old religion. The emperor Diocletian upheld Roman traditionalism with a religious fervour, as did that amazing *nouveau riche* of Greek culture, Julian the Apostate. In the later empire, indeed, one feels a sudden release of talent and creativity such as often follows the shaking of an *ancien régime*. A rising current of able men, less burdened by the prejudices of an aristocracy and eager to learn, maintained a tone of vigour and disquietude that distinguishes the intellectual climate of Late Antiquity from any other period of ancient history. Of the Fathers of the Church, for instance, only one – Ambrose (*c.* 339–97) – came from a senatorial family. The men who were able to leave their mark on the highest society of the empire had all of them made their own way from obscure towns – Plotinus (*c.* 205–70) from Upper Egypt, Augustine (354–430) from Thagaste, Jerome (*c.* 342–419) from a Stridon that he was glad to see the last of, and John Chrysostom (*c.* 347–407) from a clerk's office in Antioch. Where would this fluidity end? Would institutions less conservative than the bureaucracy and the educational system of the empire harness it more effectively? And to what disturbing ideas, long prepared in the cities of the Mediterranean, would this leavening open the way? For the moment, however, let us consider how the 'restored' society of the Roman empire, with its distinctive admixture of old and new elements, settled down to enjoy a century of comparative security.

33

The newly formed governing class that had emerged throughout the empire by 350 thought of itself as living in a world restored to order: *Reparatio Saeculi*. 'The Age of Restoration', was their favourite motto on coins and inscriptions. The fourth century is the most prosperous period of Roman rule in Britain. As soon as the emperors had pacified the Rhineland, a new aristocracy sprang up in Gaul like mushrooms after rain: men like Ausonius, who could remember how his grandfather had died as a refugee from barbarian invasion in 270, founded landed fortunes that would last for the next two centuries. In Africa and Sicily, a series of splendid mosaics illustrate the *dolce vita* of great landowners, without any significant interruption, from the third to the fifth centuries.

It is important to stress this fourth-century revival. The headlong religious and cultural changes of Late Antiquity did not take place in a world living under the shadow of a catastrophe. Far from it: they should be seen against the background of a rich and surprisingly resilient society, that had reached a balance and attained a structure significantly different from the classical Roman period.

The most blatant feature of this society, for both contemporaries and for the historian, was the widening gulf between rich and poor. In the western empire, society and culture were dominated by a senatorial aristocracy five times richer, on the average, than the senators of the first century. In the tomb of one such senator, workmen found 'a pile of golden thread' – all that remained of a typical Roman millionaire of the fourth century: Petronius Probus, 'his properties spreading all over the empire – whether honestly gotten or not', wrote a contemporary, 'is not for me to say.'

What is true of the aristocracy is true also of the urban life of the later empire. The small town shrank in importance – in Ostia, for instance, the opulent residences of the fourth-century aristocracy were built out of deserted blocks of artisan flats of the second century. But the great cities of the empire maintained their lavish style of life and high population. The quick growth of Constantinople illustrates this: founded in 324, it had 4,388 private mansions by the fifth century. Altogether, the prosperity of the Mediterranean world seems to have drained to the top: the income of a Roman senator could be as much as 120,000 gold pieces, that of a courtier at Constantinople

25 The new magnificence. Detail from the porphyry sarcophagus (*c.* AD 350) of a daughter of Constantine.

1,000; but that of a merchant only 200, and of a peasant 5 gold pieces a year.

Taxation was the greatest single cause of this change. The land-tax had trebled within living memory by 350. It reached more than one-third of a farmer's gross produce. It was inflexible and thoroughly ill-distributed. Nothing shows more clearly the ineluctable victory of the two unseen enemies of the Roman empire – time and distance. Tax assessments were conscientious; but in so huge a society they could never be either complete or frequent enough. Hence, the only way to alleviate one's burden was to evade it, leaving the less fortunate to pay up. The emperors recognized this. Occasionally they would ease the burden of taxation by spectacular gestures – privileges, remissions, the cancelling of bad debts: but these were like spouts of steam from a safety-valve; though impressive, they did nothing to redistribute the burden itself. Hence, in the western provinces of the empire, the wealth the emperor could tap shrank stealthily into the hands of great landowners, leaving the small man to have his property ground fine by the constant demands of the tax-collector: not for nothing, in the Christian hymn 'Dies Irae', is the coming of the Last Judgment thought of in terms of the arrival of a late Roman revenue official!

A society under pressure, however, is not necessarily a depressed or a rigid society. As we have seen, the society of the early fourth century was exceptionally open to currents from below – to men, to professional skills, to ideas – which the more stable world of about 200 would have dismissed as 'lower-class', 'barbarian' or 'provincial'.

The new aristocracies were, more often than not, families with strong local roots. By the fourth century, most 'senators' had never seen Rome. Instead, they were the leaders of their own society. Their official careers never took them far from their roots. They were appointed to govern those provinces in which they were already important landowners. They visited the same towns and stayed at the same villas where they passed their time as private persons. This system may have produced men with narrower horizons (although this process had long been anticipated in the social history of the empire), but it ensured that the influence of the governing classes reached down to the very bottom of provincial society. Taxes were paid and recruits appeared for the army because the great landowners ensured that their peasants did what they were told.

It was they who represented the average man in the law-courts. The great men of the locality would sit quite openly beside the judge, regulating the affairs of the community; only they now stood between the lower classes and the terrors of the tax-collectors. The remarkable petitions of peasants direct to the imperial court, such as were common in the second and early third centuries, disappear: in the late empire, all attempts to secure protection and redress of grievances had to pass through a great man – a *patronus* – 'the boss' (as in French, *le patron*), exercising his influence at court. The medieval idea of the 'patron saint', intervening on behalf of his servants at a remote and awe-inspiring Heavenly Court, is a projection upwards of this basic fact of late Roman life.

These vertical links were by no means invariably oppressive. Few late Roman men, if any, thought that their society could work in any other way: only the warmth of constant personal attention and loyalty to specific individuals could span the vast distances of the empire. The great man became the focus of intense loyalties. In Rome, for instance, the local residents regained an influence that they had lost since the republic: it was they, not the emperor, who now provided for the city. In the later empire, pictures of the aristocrat – giving games, appearing in public as a governor, even at leisure on his estate – now come to include a dense and admiring crowd.

26 The magnate in his city. A consul's triumphal procession in Rome; from the Basilica of Junius Bassus, Rome, fourth century AD.

27 Receiving largesse from Constantine. In the fourth century, distributions from the emperor and his officials largely replaced the public building by private individuals (*cf.* Ill. 3). Detail from the Arch of Constantine, Rome.

28 Watching a circus race. Crowded scenes such as this, though condemned by Christian bishops, show that the town life of the Mediterranean survived and was seen to survive up to the sixth century. Mosaic from Gafsa, Tunisia, fifth century AD.

The currents of influence in late Roman society did not only pass downwards, from top to bottom. The new élites were exceptionally open. The splendid new art of the age, for instance, is the work of craftsmen and patrons who felt themselves shaken free from the restraints of previous generations. Mass-production of standardized classical art – in sarcophagi, in copy-book mosaics, in pottery – had come to a halt in the late third century. Men now drew on what lay close to hand. Local craftsmen felt free to bring to the houses of the great new and uninhibited traditions that had already appeared in their provinces. The vigour and the expressiveness of the mosaics and statues of the fourth century show how much late Roman culture owed to a salutary dislocation and to the consequent strengthening of local roots.

38 Altogether, the society of the fourth century shows a double

30 The Palace, carefully screened from the outside world. Mosaic from Sant'Apollinare Nuovo, Ravenna, sixth century AD.

29 The country villa in Africa. Different from the sprawling, single-storeyed villa of the classical past, with a closed lower storey and towers, it could serve as a castle in times of invasion. The great landowners were increasingly expected to provide their tenants with such protection. Mosaic from Tabarka, Tunisia, fourth century A D.

PALA TIVM

movement. At the top, wealth turns inwards, the pitch of the social pyramid is heightened. This accounts for the most obvious apparent difference between late Roman and classical society – the different quality of the life of the towns. Our impression of the miraculous vigour of town life in the second century reflects a precise – and transitory – stage of the development of Roman upper-class society. At that time a group of rich men of roughly equal status, well known to each other, competed for prestige by lavishing on their home-towns buildings, statues and similar expensive and colossal *bric-à-brac*. By the fourth century, the battle for status had been fought and won: services and titles from the emperor, not the public amenities lavished on one's home-town, marked out a man; and so the great private building ventures tend to decrease. To understand the public life of a fourth-century town, we must leave the forum and the public places and go to the suburbs and to the neighbouring countryside. There we will find ourselves in a world of mosaic pavements, as magnificent as oriental carpets, by which the leading inhabitants of the late Roman town showed their undimmed affluence. The typical products of the age are the palace and the country-villa. The palaces at Ostia, for instance, are each a world of their own: arcades shrouded with curtains, walls covered with multi-coloured marbles, rainbow mosaics on the floor created an atmosphere of opulent intimacy. Even advances in plumbing are used to provide the new luxury of private bathrooms. Altogether, this was a more private, less avidly public world. In such palaces, one feels, the cultivation of friendship, of sheltered scholarship, the development of talent and religious eccentricity in the women's quarters counted for more than the 'pot-latch' public postures of a previous age.

On the other hand, a more local life had meant that certain features of Roman civilization spread much further than previously. From Bordeaux to Antioch, local aristocracies participated equally in the government of the empire: the mosaics of Rochester and Dorset show a style of life shared by country-gentlemen in Antioch and Palestine. Lower down, the humbler provincials at last came to think of themselves as 'Romans'. The development of 'Romance' languages, and hence the retreat of Celtic in Gaul and Spain, owes nothing to the classical Roman empire: it was brought about by the continued influence of the Latin-speaking landowner, tax-collector and bishop of the fourth and fifth centuries.

Many provinces participated fully in the Roman empire for the first time after the third century. The Danubian provinces, which provided the soldiers and the emperors of the 'Age of Restoration', entered Roman life with gusto: they produced fanatical Roman traditionalists, astute administrators, hard-headed and courageous heretical bishops.

Even the barbarian world was affected by this development. For an economic and cultural *glacis* no longer stood between the Mediterranean world and the military frontier of the empire. Along the Rhine and the Danube, rich villas and cosmopolitan imperial residences now stood temptingly close to the underdeveloped countries of central Europe. In some places, the boundaries of the Roman empire were hardened by this levelling-up of the *glacis*. The average Roman felt more strongly than previously that he stood alone and united against a threatening outside world; everyone within the empire could count as a *romanus*, and the empire itself was now called *Romania*. Along the Middle Rhine, however, the expansion of provincial civilization up to the frontier fostered a dangerous symbiosis of Roman and barbarian: the Alamanni who threatened Gaul from the Black Forest were already in some ways a sub-Roman society; their warriors lived in Roman-style villas and wore the same heavy belts and intricate brooches as did the Roman officers who watched over them from Cologne, Mainz and Strasbourg.

Roman civilization of the fourth century drew on a wider franchise than previously. In the East, provinces that had remained silent since the beginnings of the Hellenistic age, suddenly became seedbeds of talent. Cappadocia, proverbially a backward area, produced gifted bishop after bishop – most notable the 'Cappadocian Fathers', Basil of Caesarea (*c.* 330–79), Gregory of Nyssa (*c.* 331–96) and Gregory of Nazianze (329–89) – and flooded the classical lecture-halls of Antioch with dedicated young men. Egypt, which had been deliberately relegated to a backwater in the Roman empire, rapidly came into its own: at one and the same time the farmers of Upper Egypt created a totally new monastic culture and its towns exported a succession of gifted Greek-speaking poets.

The most decisive feature of this widening of Roman rule was, of course, that the Roman empire itself came to mean something different to the new *romani*. The old foci of loyalty had long been found to be either too abstract or too distant. Outside a restricted,

31 The emperor is arriving on horseback (as in Ill. 15), ushered in by a dancing Victory, and protected by the Christian Chi-rho emblem. This stylized silver dish, an imperial gift showing Constantius II, communicates that the emperor is always close to hand to his subjects.

32 In a late Roman court, the imperial icons hang beside the governor on his dais, and the crowd salutes them when shouting their petitions. The trial of Christ in the *Rossano Gospel*, sixth century.

if articulate, circle nostalgia for the Senate meant little; and outside the Latin world, there was no veneration for the city of Rome. Latin emperors like Diocletian and his colleagues showed that it was quite possible to be a fanatical *romanus* and yet to visit Rome only once in a lifetime. In the Greek East it was plain that the empire was the emperor. *L'état c'est moi*: this is the idea that lay behind the quite spontaneous elevation of the person of the emperor in the Late Antique period. The provincials of the eastern parts of the empire were enthusiastic 'Romans'. They called themselves *Rhomaioi* for the next thousand years; and in the medieval Near East the Byzantine empire was always known as *Rūm*, 'Rome', and Christians as 'Romans', *Rūmi*. But the provincials felt this loyalty, not through the brittle protocol of senatorial or civic institutions, but directly – by falling on their knees before statues and icons of the emperor himself, whose majestic pose and searching eyes brought home to them the only man whose 'ceaseless, many-sided care' embraced all the inhabitants of *Romania*.

A vital difference between the western and the eastern parts of the empire is betrayed by this difference in loyalty. In the East, there

were more participants in the empire, and more prosperous participants, than in the West. Because of this, enthusiasm for the emperor struck firmer roots in the eastern empire, and so took this more uninhibitedly popular form.

Ever since the conquests of the Roman republic, large areas of the West had remained overwhelmingly agricultural and largely underdeveloped. Such a primitive economy could not stand the complex repercussions of a century of unprecedented taxation. By the fifth century, the wealth of the West had snowballed into the hands of a few great families: an oligarchy of senators stood between the average man and the imperial government in every province. In the East, the greater importance of trade, and the proliferation of small but viable cities in the hinterland of the Mediterranean, ensured a more balanced, even a more egalitarian society. The local landowners of a Greek city might be very rich and very conservative, but, while Gaul and Italy fell into the hands of half a dozen great clans, ten families at least competed for influence round Antioch alone. The gains of a Greek civic magnate remained limited to his locality, and the city itself remained the focus of his energies. The Greek idea of *euergeia*, of

43

a rivalry of great houses in showing good for their community, was remarkably resilient. In the mid-fifth century a bishop, when accused of heresy, would instinctively defend himself in terms of this tradition: what could the local notables have against him; had he not embellished their city by building an aqueduct and the public porticoes? Such an evenly balanced gentry was never overshadowed and cowed by overmighty landowners: they provided an unfailing reservoir of well-educated and conscientious civil servants for the administration in Constantinople, and throughout the late Roman period they decorated their towns with statues, inscriptions and churches whose richness is only beginning to be discovered by archaeologists in Turkey.

Furthermore, the peasants of Asia Minor, Syria and Egypt were very different from the dragooned and excluded serfs of the western provinces. They could get a good enough price for their corn in the towns to pay both their rent and their taxes. They could, therefore, meet the demands of the government without being shepherded on to the estates of the great landowners. In the middle of the fifth century, the difference in atmosphere between the two parts of the empire was largely due to the different role of the small man. When Gaul was being terrorized by peasants' revolts, provoked by taxation and rack-renting, the farmers of northern Syria were able to build substantial stone houses in villages that now shelter only a few nomads; the tenants of Palestine had maintained a hydraulic system that made the Lake of Galilee and the Negev a garden strewn with gay mosaic pavements; the peasants of Egypt were finding expression for their stubborn independence and ingenuity in the great monastic encampments of the Thebaid. The parting of the ways between western Europe and the eastern Mediterranean, which is the most important immediate legacy of the Late Antique world, goes back to such humble, concrete contrasts.

Two towns of the fourth and fifth centuries have recently been excavated – Ostia (near Rome) and Ephesus (Efes, Turkey). Both have surprised the scholar by the resilience of the old world in their architecture, and in the traces of their civic life. The mosaics of Ostia may point the way to medieval art; but they are equally tenaciously linked to the colourful traditions of first-century Pompeii and Herculaneum. Like many phenomena of the later Roman empire, only a trick of perspective makes them appear totally unrelated to the classical world. Classical scholars have concentrated so much on the first century of the Roman empire that they tend to forget the long, quiet transformation of classical art, and of the classical forms of public life, in the two centuries between Trajan and Constantine.

Two features would never have appeared at any earlier time. Both towns have a series of stylized statues whose immobile features and raised eyes betray a new preoccupation with the inner life and with the supernatural. Both towns have large Christian basilicas. These features are a reminder that, however well the men of the fourth-century 'Age of Restoration' may have adjusted themselves to a new political and social situation, seismic shifts in their religion and culture stood between them and the classical world of 200. To understand these shifts we must go back in time to the age of Marcus Aurelius; we must embrace different sections of experience; we must even consider different areas of Roman society, so as to trace the religious changes of the second, third and fourth centuries in intellectuals and religious leaders, and in the hopes and disquietudes of the average inhabitant of the great Mediterranean cities.

33 A late Roman town: Antioch in the fourth century. Detail from a mosaic, the 'Mepalopsychia Hunt'.

34, 35 The new idiom. Local craftsmen and their patrons felt free to abandon classical canons of taste. They preferred a vigorous, abstract approach to the human figure (as on the fourth-century tomb-mosaic at Tabarka, North Africa, *left*), and they brought an element of fairy-tale into stock themes of classical mythology (as in the mosaic of Orpheus and the Beasts, from a fifth-century pavement in Palestine, *right*).

IV THE NEW MOOD: DIRECTIONS OF RELIGIOUS THOUGHT,
c. 170–300

The historian is in danger of forgetting that his subjects spent much of their time asleep, and that, when asleep, they had dreams. One Greek rhetor, however, Aelius Aristides (118–80), has left us a full account of his dreams. He recorded them as *Sacred Tales*, for these dreams deal primarily with appearances of the god Asclepius. They include dreams of religious terror and exaltation. Aristides became convinced that he was the elect of the god and that his waking life was a 'divine drama' moulded at every step by the loving care of Asclepius.

The case of Aristides reminds us, should this be necessary, that the Roman empire at the height of its prosperity had room for many such eccentrics: we are dealing with a society in which the overwhelming majority of educated men had always turned, not to philosophy, even less to science, but rather to the means made available to them by their traditional religion, to cope with the business of living.

Yet it is equally important to notice that the intense dream-life of Aristides made not the slightest difference to his determination to live a successful life as a conservative, educated gentleman: Asclepius merely helped him through the 'breakdowns' that might have threatened his successful career. We know him as the author of a classic panegyric on the benefits of the Roman empire, and as a bitter enemy of the Christians – 'men in Palestine who show their impiety as you would expect them to, by having no respect for their betters'.

Aristides still felt firmly held in a traditional pagan life. In the century following Aristides, a change was to come about. The rich religious life of the Mediterranean, which had shown an infinite capacity to draw on the exotic and the eccentric, suddenly ebbed away from the traditional mould in which men like Aristides felt entirely at home. Many tried to reinterpret their ancestral religion; a few obtained 'a divorce from the ways of the past' by becoming

49

36 The new mood. 'I shall lift up mine eyes to the hills, from whence cometh my help.' Fourth-century portrait of a deceased woman, from the Catacomb of Vigna Massimo, Rome.

Christians. The period between about 170 and the conversion of the emperor Constantine to Christianity in 312 saw a vast and anxious activity in religion. We have the first literary duels between Christian and educated pagans: the pagan Celsus wrote his *True Doctrine* in about 168, and was answered at length by Origen of Alexandria in 248. In their cultivated study-groups, Gnostic teachers attempted to plumb the depths of the 'true knowledge', the *gnosis*, contained in Christianity. (Writings of Gnostics, of about 170, have recently been discovered in a Coptic translation at Nag-Hammadi, Egypt.) Pagans cast their disquietudes into the form of little treatises of edification, such as the revelations of the Egyptian Hermes Trismegistos, the 'Thrice-great Hermes'.

It would be naïve to regard the changes betrayed in these writings merely as the decline of a classical enlightenment and the rise of super-stition. The starting-point in the age of the Antonines is not so much enlightenment as the diffused and well-regulated superstition by which many a well-rooted and successful governing class persuades itself that it lives in as good a world as possible. The attitude is sum-med up in the motto that frequently occurs on coins of the second and third centuries: *Providentia deorum* – 'The gods are looking after us'. 'The gods are always there to show their power', Marcus Aurelius wrote, 'They help us in their marvellous way. They send us dreams; they reveal mysteries; they provide us with remedies against ill-health, and oracles for our uncertainties.'

Educated pagans still felt at home in their universe. According to the philosophers, the universe was ruled by One High God, who was quite inexpressible and thus 'above' everything. This one God, how-ever, was fully represented on earth by the ministrations of the many gods of traditional belief. These were thought of as His 'ministering spirits': they were the provincial governors of His far-flung empire. The average man was quite content with these homely figures, and the dress of the classical Olympians still fitted them. There was no period of the ancient world in which the average man could be quite as certain that he knew exactly what the classical gods looked like: they were everywhere in the second century, in their most stereotyped and traditional form – on mass-produced statues, coins and pottery.

These gods were believed to care for mankind in general, and for cities and individuals in particular. The case of Aristides shows how seriously people expected direct personal attention. Throughout the Roman world, cities and individuals were giving the old gods every opportunity to look after their worshippers: the second century saw a remarkable revival of the traditional oracle-sites of the Greek world.

This care was obtained by following rites regarded as being as old as the human race itself. To abandon such rites provoked genuine anxiety and hatred. Christians were savagely attacked for having neglected these rites whenever earthquakes, famine or barbarian invasion betrayed the anger of the gods.

Altogether, in such a system of belief, a man could feel embedded in the closely knit structure of a world permeated by the care of age-old gods. He could feel certain that what his parents and his fellows had always done in their home-towns fitted without tension into the vast enveloping mass of a perfect universe. Traditional belief in the activity of the gods in the universe presented a singularly unified and unbroken surface. The thoughts and anxieties of the 'new mood' after 170 drove fissures across it. It is by examining some of the new preoccupations of sensitive men that we can appreciate the nature of the spiritual revolution that makes Late Antiquity such a distinct and fertile period in the history of the ancient Mediterranean.

First, the individual had a growing sense of possessing something in himself that was infinitely valuable and yet painfully unrelated to the outside world. After generations of apparently satisfying public activity, it was as if a current that had passed smoothly from men's inner experience into the outside world had been cut. The warmth drained from the familiar environment. Traditional concerns seemed trivial, if not positively oppressive. Already Marcus Aurelius looks at the world as if through the small end of a telescope: the Danubian campaigns by which he saved the empire in 172–75 and 178–80 strike him as 'puppies fighting for a bone'. We find the philosopher Plotinus wondering: 'When I come to myself, I wonder how it is that I have a body . . . by what deterioration did this happen?' The Gnostic 'awakens' to find life is a nightmare 'in which we flee one knows not where, or else remain inert in pursuit of one knows not whom'. The baptized Christian stands as a 'son of God', pitched against a world ruled by a prince of evil.

Finding a sudden reserve of perfection or inspiration inside oneself went hand in hand with a need for a God with whom one could be alone: a God whose 'charge', as it were, had remained concentrated and personal rather than diffused in benign but profoundly impersonal ministrations to the universe at large. Men who still felt that it was their conventional activities that needed to be blessed or stimulated were opaque to this new need: Aristides felt utterly dependent on Asclepius, but he was predictably conventional in regarding Zeus as the distant ruler of a thoroughly Greek pantheon. The new mood, by contrast, appealed straight to the centre and away from the subordinate gods of popular belief – to the One God Himself, as a figure of latent, unexpressed power. For the Gnostics, for instance, the good God had been utterly hidden, had never been known before; he had made a sudden 'breakthrough', in order to appear, at last, to the believer from behind the towering machinery of a diabolical world. In various ways the reassuring age-old imagery of minor gods that had swaddled the One God of the *bien pensant* was stripped away. The Christian found himself face to face with the drastic simplicity of the one 'God of the Universe'; and even for the thinking pagan the Olympians had begun to seem a little transparent. The classical mask no longer fitted over the looming and inscrutable core of the universe.

It would be naïve to describe this development merely as a growth of 'otherworldliness'. Far from it: the belief that one could be in direct contact with something bigger than oneself was no small help in a time of revolutionary change; and it was not in the least inconsistent with political acumen. Traditional paganism had expressed itself through forms as impersonal as the universe itself: it mobilized feelings for sacred *things* – for ancient rites, for statues, for oracles, for vast beloved temples. The 'new mood', by contrast, threw up men – raw individuals who believed that they were the agents of vast forces. The men who really left their mark on the Roman world in the third and fourth centuries all believed that they were acting as 'servants' of God or of the gods, and drew lavishly on the supernatural for guidance and sanction in a puzzling age: ecclesiastical organizers such as Cyprian, bishop of Carthage (248–58); reforming emperors – Aurelian (270–75) the pagan, Constantine the Christian, Julian the Apostate (361–63); fertile and pertinacious geniuses, such as St Athanasius (c. 296–373) and St Augustine.

The sense of an imminent 'breakthrough' of divine energy in the inner world of the individual had revolutionary effects. For innumerable humble men and women it subtly loosened the moulding power of classical culture and of the habitual sanctions of behaviour. Pagan and Christian writings of the 'new mood' share an interest in 'conversion' in its sharpest sense – that is, they regarded it as possible for the 'real' divine self suddenly to emerge at the expense of the individual's normal social identity. The 'reborn' pupil of Thrice-Great Hermes, the 'spiritual' man of the Gnostics, the baptized Christian, each felt that a glass wall stood between his new life and his past: his new behaviour owed everything to God and nothing to society.

The idea of 'conversion' was closely related to the idea of 'revelation'. Between them, the two ideas opened a breach in the high wall of classical culture for the average man. By 'conversion' he gained a moral excellence which had previously been reserved for the classical Greek and Roman gentleman because of his careful grooming and punctilious conformity to ancient models. By 'revelation' the uneducated might get to the heart of vital issues, without exposing himself to the high costs, to the professional rancours and to the heavy traditionalism of a second-century education in philosophy. Pagan philosophers, who might share many aspects of the 'new mood', were bitterly opposed to Christians and to pagan Gnostics who relied on such means. 'Revelation', for a philosopher such as Plotinus, was not merely irrational: it led to second-rate counterfeits of traditional academic philosophical culture. It was as if the inhabitants of an underdeveloped country were to seek to catch up with western technology by claiming to have learnt nuclear physics through dreams and oracles.

Men who had discovered some inner perfection in themselves, who felt capable of intimate contact with the One God, found the problem of evil, also, to be more intimate, more drastic. To 'look at the sum total of things', to treat human miseries with detachment – as so many regrettable traffic-accidents on the well-regulated road system of the universe – was plainly insufficient. It made no sense of the vigour of conflicting emotions within oneself. Hence the most crucial development of these centuries: the definitive splitting-off of the 'demons' as active forces of evil, against whom men had to pit themselves. The sharp smell of an invisible battle hung over the religious and intellectual life of Late Antique man. To sin was no longer merely to err: it was to allow oneself to be overcome by unseen forces. To err

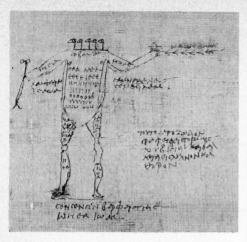

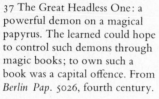

37 The Great Headless One: a
powerful demon on a magical
papyrus. The learned could hope
to control such demons through
magic books; to own such a
book was a capital offence. From
Berlin Pap. 5026, fourth century.

was not to be mistaken: it was to be unconsciously manipulated by
some invisible malign power. The more strongly people felt about
their ideas, the more potent the demons seemed to them: Christians
believed that traditional paganism, far from being the work of men,
was an 'opium of the masses', pumped into the human race by the
non-human demons; and one scholar even ascribed bad reviews of
his book to demonic inspiration!

But if the demons were the 'stars' of the religious drama of Late
Antiquity, they needed an impresario. They found this in the Christian
Church. Outside Christianity, the demons had remained ambivalent
(rather like ghosts). They were invoked to explain sudden and in-
congruous misfortunes, deviations from normative behaviour such
as riots, plagues and inappropriate love-affairs. They were as widely
invoked, and caused as little anxiety, as microbes do today. Christianity, however, made the demons central to its view of the world.
The Christian Church had inherited, through late Judaism, that most
fateful legacy of Zoroastrian Persia to the western world – a belief
in the absolute division of the spiritual world between good and evil
powers, between angels and demons. To men increasingly preoccupied with the problem of evil, the Christian attitude to the

38 (*left*) Driving out the demon. At an abrupt word of command from a holy man, the demon visibly leaves the sufferer. Relief from the bronze door of the Church of San Zeno, Verona, twelfth century.

39 Miracles of healing. For the average man, Christ was a wonder-worker. Even pagans revered Him as a redoubtable magician. Detail from an Italian ivory diptych, 450–60.

demons offered an answer designed to relieve nameless anxiety: they focused this anxiety on the demons and at the same time offered a remedy for it. The devil was given vast but strictly mapped-out powers. He was an all-embracing agent of evil in the human race; but he had been defeated by Christ and could be held in check by Christ's human agents. The Christians were convinced that they were merely 'mopping-up', on earth, a battle that had already been won for them in Heaven. The monks treated the demons with the delighted alarm of small boys visiting a lion in the zoo; and the Christian bishops set about their work in the heady frame of mind of many a revolutionary – they faced a diabolically organized society that was, at one and the same time, towering, noxious, and yet hollow, doomed to destruction. Hence, however many sound social and cultural reasons the historian may find for the expansion of the Christian Church, the fact remains that in all Christian literature from the New Testament onwards, the Christian missionaries advanced principally by revealing the bankruptcy of men's invisible enemies, the demons, through exorcisms and miracles of healing.

Nothing reveals more clearly the brisk and pugnacious climate that developed in the third century than the role allotted to the

55

demons. They came to be identified as intrusive elements of evil in every situation of disease and misfortune. Yet their presence did not weigh as heavily on Late Antique men as we might think, precisely because they could be 'isolated' and driven out. In disease, for instance, the holy man could 'see' the demon in the human body, and could expel it, often in the satisfactorily concrete form of a visible object – as a mouse, a reptile, a bird. Thus, one of the most profound and mysterious changes in men's attitude to themselves took place. In the age of the Antonines, we meet a surprising number of florid vale-tudinarians: Aelius Aristides made constant capital out of his ill-health; and Galen, the doctor (c. 129–99), was the intellectual leader of Roman society. Their hypochondria is a puzzling and disturbing symptom; but it was expressed in terms of the traditional views of Greek medicine – men focused their anxieties on the imbalance of humours in their own bodies. Men of later generations tended to disown disease as springing from themselves: defence against attacks by demons preoccupied them more than did the intimate disorders of their constitutions.

Altogether, the 'new mood' encouraged men to feel that they needed to defend their identity by drawing sharp boundaries round it. They fitted less easily into their communities and felt out of place in the physical world. They stood aloof and alone with their One God. By conversion, by accepting a revelation, they cut themselves off from their own past and from the beliefs of the mass of their fellows. They manned the barricades in an invisible battle with the demons. As a result, the individual came to feel more strongly than ever previously that he needed to survive in another, better existence. The third century saw an increase in the influence of religious groups who claimed that their members, who had to defend with such ferocity a new-won sense of uniqueness in this world, would enjoy victory and rest in the next. The initiate of Mithras, for instance, was armed against the demons, who might attack his soul as it rose to Heaven after death, through the tranquil glow of the Milky Way. The paint-ings of the Christian catacombs express similar ideas. By baptism the believer was 'snatched' from the dangers of this world: he was identified with Daniel, standing peacefully, his arms outstretched in prayer, in the middle of the lions' den. After death he enjoyed a Heavenly 'repose' – *refrigerium* – as Jonah had once rested from the cruel heat of the day in the cool of an arbour.

The most profound boundary in the Late Antique world was the one drawn after death. The invisible chasm between the 'saved' and the 'damned' stood like a deep moat round the little groups, pagan and Christian alike, that came to chisel out a position for themselves at the expense of the time-honoured consensus of traditional public worship.

The age of the Antonines saw the coming together of these thoughts. Hence the strange appearance of that age. Reading the literature of the classical upper classes we can agree with Gibbon: 'If a man were called to fix the period in the history of the world, during which the condition of the human race was most happy and prosperous, he would, without hesitation, name that which elapsed from the death of Domitian to the accession of Commodus' – for in this, he was accepting the judgment of a group of contemporaries on themselves. Traditional civic life had never spread so far in western Europe. In the Greek world, a new self-confidence expressed itself in a romantic revival of classical culture and religion. Men still felt at ease in their cities. The heroes of the age were not saints: they were the 'Sophists' – orators who played a vital role in the life of the towns (see p. 17). The leading professor of rhetoric in Rome received 100,000 sesterces a year.

At exactly the same time, a Christian bishop in Rome was receiving only 7,000 sesterces a year. To all appearances, his group was dwarfed by the robust edifice of classical public life; he was an incomprehensible emigrant in a great city, like Karl Marx in Victorian London. Yet one can already see why, in the next century, the Christian bishop might emerge from oblivion: for one traditional star-orator there had already sprung up in Rome a dozen little conventicles, the *didaskaleia* – the study-groups – of questioning men. There was the Christian Church proper; the conventicles of the Gnostic Valentinus, 'the children of the understanding of the heart'; the hushed lecture-hall atmosphere of the disciples of Thrice-Great Hermes. In the next chapter we shall see why it was that, when the flamboyant public life of the ancient cities was touched by the frost of public emergency after 240, a world obscurely prepared among humble men in such little conventicles was able to come to the fore in the form of an organized Christian Church.

★

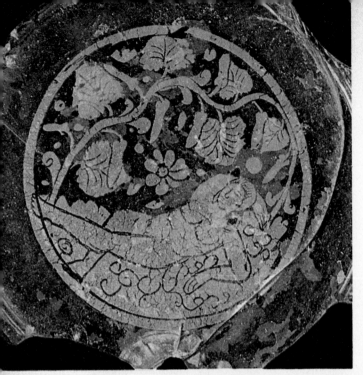

40 The imagery of the afterlife. The rest of Jonah in the shade of a gourd (compare the dirge in Shakespeare's *Cymbeline*, 'Fear no more the heat of the sun'). Fourth-century gold-leaf glass.

41 Death was not only rest. It was also a lucky escape from the dangers of this world and the next; Vibia is here led by a Good Angel to a heavenly banquet. Fourth-century wall painting from pagan tomb of Vibia, Rome.

43 The religious leaders. This second-century wall painting from Dura-Europos shows the appeal of the East in the person of a Persian priest. Zoroaster was treated as one of the wise men of the classical world, and the 'Persian philosophy' continued to attract even such very Greek thinkers as Plotinus.

42 (*above*) The philosopher and his praying convert. As a director, the 'man of culture' can even save souls. From a sarcophagus in S. Maria Antiqua, Rome.

44 The study group. Here the teacher is alone with his little band of disciples. Fourth-century wall painting in the Catacomb of the Via Latina, Rome.

In few ages has one-half of the world lived in such stalwart indifference to how the other half was living as in the Roman empire of the second century. Rome, as Disraeli was to say of Victorian England, was 'two nations'. The traditional governing classes prided themselves on preserving the ancient particularities of their home-towns. The Athenians, for instance, completed the temple of Olympian Zeus at the instigation of the emperor Hadrian, after a lapse of a mere 638 years! They used expensive and unnecessary T-clamps to copy exactly the buildings of the fifth century B C. The Greek aristocracies treasured their local rites and priesthoods as guarantees of local status, and through a fear that the vast empire in which they found themselves would become a cultural dust-bowl. They insisted on seeing the Roman world as a mosaic of distinct cities and tribes. The general attitude of the age stressed the brittle honeycomb of local patriotisms: the Greek cities produced a rash of coins, each honouring its own god; and an African city summed it up in an inscription – 'More power to the home-town!'

At exactly the same time, however, it was possible for a young student, Tatian, to pass from the eastern, Syrian fringe of the Roman empire to Rome, speaking Greek all the way and participating in a uniform Greek philosophical culture. He returned home disgruntled – and a Christian. The strident particularism of the cities of the empire had shocked him. Each had its own laws; each was ruled by a narrow oligarchy. 'There should be one code of law for all mankind,' he wrote, 'and one political organization.'

Tatian spoke for thousands of men whose experience of the Roman empire was diametrically opposite to that of its dominant classes. To the articulate Roman and Greek gentleman, the peace of the empire had come as an opportunity to fortify and cherish the customs of one's ancient town. To humbler men it meant nothing of the sort: it meant wider horizons and unprecedented opportunities for travel; it meant the erosion of local differences through trade and emigration, and the weakening of ancient barriers before new wealth and new criteria of status. Imperceptibly, the Roman empire dissolved in the lower classes that sense of tradition and local loyalties on which its upper class depended.

While the Greek cities of the Aegean coast of Asia Minor were priding themselves on having maintained their local characteristics

45 Christianity as seen by a pagan. A crucified donkey with 'Alexander is worshipping his god'. Second-century graffito.

(even their local feuds!) since the fifth century B C, the inhabitants of their hinterland – in Phrygia, Bithynia, Cappadocia – had entered a new world. Their merchants were constantly on the move, seeking opportunities in the underdeveloped territories of western Europe, often settling far from their native towns. One Phrygian merchant, for instance, visited Rome seventy-two times in his life.

It is precisely the men who were being uprooted and cast adrift from their old life who provided the background to the anxious thoughts of the religious leaders of the late second century. The successful businessman, the freedman administrator, the woman whose status and education had slowly improved, found themselves no longer citizens of their accustomed town, but 'citizens of the world'; and many, it appears, were finding that the world was a lonely and impersonal place. It is among such people that we find the Christians. By 200 the Christian communities were not recruited from among the 'humble and oppressed': they were groupings of the lower middle classes and of the respectable artisans of the cities. Far from being deprived, these people had found fresh opportunities and prosperity in the Roman empire: but they also had to devise ways of dealing with the anxieties and uncertainties of their new position.

46, 47 The group. Solemn little banquets were a normal feature of ancient life. Families had always eaten beside the graves of their dead relatives; and so, by eating together, pagan or Christian worshippers treated each other as members of a single religious family. Third-century wall paintings from the Catacomb of SS. Pietro e Marcellino and the Catacomb of Priscilla, Rome.

It is one of the fascinations of the archaeology of the Roman empire that we can see so clearly some of the ways in which simple, self-respecting men tried to regulate their behaviour, to choose objects of worship, to create human relationships, in towns that had become more cosmopolitan, less intimate, where the old landmarks were fading.

The spread of the oriental cults in western Europe, for instance, is a notorious feature of the first and second centuries. These cults spread because they gave the immigrant, and later the local adherent, a sense of belonging, a sense of loyalty that he lacked in the civic functions of his town. There is touching evidence of the spontaneous growth of little clubs of the well-to-do poor. One would dine with fellow members when living, and be buried and remembered by them when dead. In a more sinister way, a proliferation of manuals of astrology, of dream-books, of books of sorcery, show with how much anxiety a new public of half-educated men needed to feel in control of a life whose pace had quickened.

In all this, the outlook of the upper classes of the Roman world ran counter to the experience of the more prosperous plebeians in the towns. The philosophical culture of the Greek world had reached its maximum diffusion; but at just that time, the Greek upper classes were abandoning a flexible, living Greek, the *Koiné* that had been the lingua franca of the whole East, in favour of an archaic Attic style which could only be spoken by a meticulously educated élite. When asked how he would punish a brigand, a contemporary rhetor remarked, 'Make him learn the ancient classics by heart, as I have to do.' The élite, therefore, was erecting a high bulwark round its own culture, and so implicitly disenfranchized a turbulent intellectual proletariat. The Gnostic and Hermetic literatures show how avidly people still wished to appropriate Greek philosophical culture, in order to solve their urgent problems: and, if they could not go to the professors to get it, they would go to religious leaders, in whose mouths the platitudes of many a dusty lecture-room would strike the new inquirer with the spontaneity and simplicity of a 'revelation'. Already some writers looked down from the high battlements of their classical culture at the obscure world pressing in upon them: Galen (who, significantly, found his own profession of medicine flooded with enthusiastic illiterates) noticed that the Christians were apparently enabled by their brutally simple parables and commands to live according to the highest maxims of ancient ethics. The Christian Apologists boasted of just this achievement. Plato, they said, had served good food with fancy dressings, but the Apostles cooked for the masses in a wholesome soup-kitchen! The social history of 'middlebrow' culture in the Roman world was on the side of the Apologists, not of Galen: a new half-educated public had turned away from the great Platonic dialogues to more simple fare, provided by homespun philosophers such as Epictetus, and by handbooks of Pythagorean maxims.

The well-to-do plebeians even patronized a new art, freed from the restraints of the classical models on the forum and in the temples. This was an art designed to convey a message: schematic, impressionistic, with formalized meaningful gestures, the faces of the figures turned towards the spectator so as to be fully recognizable. Like so much of the religion and culture of Late Antiquity, the distinctive 'Late Antique' style of the art of the fourth century was not a totally new departure: it has its roots in a culture obscurely prepared in the two preceding centuries, by humble men who still lived in the shadow of exclusive aristocracies.

The rise of Christianity cannot be isolated from the social changes we have been describing. The expansion of Christianity was not a gradual, ineluctable process beginning with St Paul and ending with the conversion of Constantine in 312. Its expansion in the third century was impressive, because it had been totally unexpected. Very suddenly, the Christian Church became a force to be reckoned with in the Mediterranean towns. The very seriousness of the measures taken against the Church as a body, and not merely against individual Christians, in the persecutions of 257 and after 303, shows that something was lacking in the life of a Roman town, which Christianity was threatening to fulfil.

The Christian Church differed from the other oriental cults, which it resembled in so many other ways, through its intolerance of the outside world. The cults were exclusive and, often, the jealously guarded preserve of foreigners; but they never set themselves up against the traditional religious observances of the society round them. They never enjoyed the publicity of intermittent persecution. While the oriental cults provided special means to salvation in the next world, they took the position of their devotees in this world for granted. The Christian Church offered a way of living in this world. The skilful elaboration of the ecclesiastical hierarchy, the sense of belonging to a distinctive group with carefully prescribed habits and increasing resources heightened the impression that the Christian Church made on the uncertain generations of the third century. Seldom has a small minority played so successfully on the anxieties of society as did the Christians. They remained a small group: but they succeeded in becoming a big problem.

Christian missionaries made most headway in just those areas where Roman society was most fluid. The seedbeds of the Church were the raw new provinces of the hinterland of Asia Minor. In a province such as Lycaonia, the arrival of Greek civilization had virtually coincided with the arrival of St Paul. The religious leader Marcion, who brought the Christian community in Rome some 200,000 sesterces, was a contemporary from the same region as the Phrygian merchant who had made this journey seventy-two times.

It is part of the appeal of a religious group that it can be a little ahead of social developments. It was possible to achieve in a small group, 'among the brethren', relationships that were being achieved in society at large at a heavy cost of conflict and uncertainty. As a member of a church, the Christian could cut some of the more painful Gordian knots of social living. He could, for instance, become a radical cosmopolitan. His literature, his beliefs, his art and his jargon were extraordinarily uniform, whether he lived in Rome, Lyons, Carthage or Smyrna. The Christians were immigrants at heart – ideological *déracinés*, separated from their environment by a belief which they knew they shared with little groups all over the empire. At a time when so many local barriers were being painfully and obscurely eroded, the Christians had already taken the step of calling themselves a 'non-nation'.

The Church was also professedly egalitarian. A group in which there was 'neither slave nor free' might strike an aristocrat as utopian, or subversive. Yet in an age when the barriers separating the successful freedman from the *déclassé* senator were increasingly unreal, a religious group could take the final step of ignoring them. In Rome the Christian community of the early third century was a place where just such anomalies were gathered and tolerated: the Church included a powerful freedman chamberlain of the emperor; its bishop was the former slave of that freedman; it was protected by the emperor's mistress, and patronized by noble ladies.

For men whose confusions came partly from no longer feeling embedded in their home environment, the Christian Church offered a drastic experiment in social living, reinforced by the excitements and occasional perils of a break with one's past and one's neighbours.

This intense sense of the religious community was the legacy of Judaism. It saved the Christian Church. Because it thought of itself as 'the true Israel', the Christian community was able to remain rooted in every town in which it was established, like a limpet on a rock when the tide recedes. In the late third century, the public religious ceremonies of the towns diminished; the dislocation of trade starved the oriental cults of immigrant devotees; but the Christian bishop remained, with a stable community and a long past behind him, to reap his harvest in the towns.

The wealth of the local notables was not so much impaired by the crisis of the late third century, as redirected: sums of money that had been spent on the townsfolk in the previous century were invested in more private living and on more frankly egotistical forms of competition for status. Naturally, the gods were affected by this change in the tempo of social life. Public competition in the second century had involved a large amount of religious activity – rites, processions, dedications of statues and temples. The Late Antique style of life, by contrast, was more blatantly personal, and so more secular: a magnate spent lavishly, but he gave shows and processions in order to emphasize his personal standing, his *potentia*; he did not care for reinforcing communal activities, such as religious festivals. Not surprisingly, therefore, the lavish inscriptions in honour of the traditional gods come to a halt after 250.

The Christian community suddenly came to appeal to men who felt deserted. At a time of inflation, the Christians invested large sums of liquid capital in people; at a time of increased brutality, the courage of Christian martyrs was impressive; during public emergencies, such as plague or rioting, the Christian clergy were shown to be the only united group in the town, able to look after the burial of the dead and to organize food-supplies. In Rome, the Church was supporting fifteen hundred poor and widows by 250. The churches of Rome and Carthage were able to send large sums of money to Africa and Cappadocia, to ransom Christian captives after barbarian raids in 254 and 256. Two generations previously, the Roman state, faced by similar problems after an invasion, had washed its hands of the poorer provincials: the lawyers declared that even Roman citizens would have to remain the slaves of the private individuals who bought them back from the barbarians. Plainly, to be a Christian in 250 brought more protection from one's fellows than to be a *civis romanus*.

But the true measure of the crisis of the towns is not to be found in the appeal of a few spectacular public gestures by the Christian Church. What marked the Christian Church off, and added to its appeal, was the ferociously inward-looking quality of its life. The Church did not scatter its alms indiscriminately: collected from the Christian community, they were presented by the bishop to God as the special 'sacrifice' of the group. (The 'sacrifice' of alms was quite as much part of the sacrificial offering of the Christians as was the Eucharist; this, in itself, was a most significant departure from pagan practice.) Thus blessed, the wealth of the community returned to the members of the community alone, as part of the 'loving-kindness' of God to His special people.

Nor was Christian propaganda indiscriminate. The Christians did not adopt the market-place preaching of the Cynic philosophers. Instead, applicants for membership were supposed to be carefully scrutinized; they were slowly prepared for initiation; and, once initiated, a formidable penitential system made them constantly aware of the awesome chasm between belonging and not belonging to the religious group.

In the mid-third century, an educated Roman, Cyprian of Carthage, could simply disappear into this exotic and self-contained world. From 248 to 258 he spent the last part of his life performing feats of organization and diplomacy in order to maintain the Christian 'faction' in Carthage. The appeal of Christianity still lay in its radical sense of community: it absorbed people because the individual could drop from a wide impersonal world into a miniature community, whose demands and relations were explicit.

The Christian Church enjoyed complete tolerance between 260 and 302. This, the 'Little Peace of the Church', was of crucial importance, as we shall see (on p. 82), for the future development of Christianity in the Roman empire. As for the emperors, they were too preoccupied with the frontiers to care about the Christians. This is a sign of how far away the Rhine and the Danube were from the heart of the classical world; for a generation, the emperors and their advisers turned their backs on what was happening in the Mediterranean cities. When Diocletian finally established his palace in Nicomedia in 287, he was able to look out at a basilica of the Christians standing on the opposite hill. The Roman empire had survived; but in this Roman empire, Christianity had come to stay.

48 The art of the humble. A simple message: a woman prays, the dove brings an olive branch, the symbol of peace. Graffito found on a tombstone from the Catacombs.

49 The philosopher. 'The very pupils of his eyes were winged, he had a long grey beard; one could hardly endure the sharp movement of his eyes.' This description of the philosopher who most influenced Julian the Apostate fits this portrait head from Ephesus, fifth century.

In 268, a war-band of Heruls from across the Danube raided Athens. They were beaten off by the men of Attica themselves, headed by the historian Dexippus (*fl.* 253–76). Life returned to a damaged city. The famous Agora stood deserted; improvised walls ringed the Acropolis. Yet Dexippus does not mention this incident in his public inscription: what mattered for him was that he had duly celebrated the Pan-Athenian Games. By the mid-fourth century Athens was once again a thriving university city. When the young prince, Julian, visited it as a student, he found that philosophy had risen again all over Greece, like a periodic flooding of the Nile. A century and a half after Julian, when the Christians robbed the Parthenon of its statues, the philosopher Proclus (411–85) dreamt that the goddess Athene stood beside him and asked if 'his Lady Athene might have shelter in his lodgings'.

The history of Athens illustrates an important facet of the civilization of Late Antiquity. In this period, tenacious survivals, regroupings of traditional forces and rediscoveries of the past are quite as important as the radical changes we have just been describing. Future ages were to owe as much to the revivals as to the innovations of the Late Antique period.

The intelligentsia of the Greek world had lived a sheltered life in the third century. At the nadir of the public fortunes of the empire, in the 260s, the philosopher Plotinus had been able to settle down undisturbed in a Campanian villa, patronized by Roman senators; and pupils came to him from Egypt, Syria and Arabia. Later, in the fourth and fifth centuries, pagan philosophers and rhetors throve in towns beside the Aegean that were still bathed in the memory of Greece. More even than in the case of the landed aristocracy, we are dealing with a world of long traditions, that changed slowly and had merely regrouped itself, without any break with the past.

These men called themselves 'the Hellenes', and their beliefs 'Hellenism'. They had restored the threatened citadel of authentic Greek wisdom. By the end of the third century, they had decisively turned back that great barbarian raid of the spirit – Gnosticism. The black counterfeit Platonism of the Gnostics had attracted intellectuals of a previous generation; but far from becoming more pessimistic, more inclined to reject the physical world, the men of the late third century shook this dark mood from themselves, and never looked

50 The survival of the gods. A Byzantine calendar shows the universe ruled by the Sun God, with diadem, holding the globe of the world. All the divine forces radiate from this centre, passing through the planets and the zodiac in an ordered and readily intelligible progression, to influence human affairs. For the medieval astronomer, as for the emperor Julian the Apostate, the sun remained 'the King'. Illumination from the Vatican copy of Ptolemy's *Astronomy*, made between 813 and 820.

back. The defeat of Gnosticism in intellectual circles is a striking example of the ability of the aristocratic culture of Late Antiquity to break a movement which had seemed, a century earlier, to be leading to a wholesale *trahison des clercs*.

Up to the end of the sixth century, a large circle of 'Hellenes' held their own against that 'barbarian theosophy' – Christianity. It is a tribute to their prestige that, in the Greek world, 'Hellene' was the word for 'pagan'. Hence a paradox in east Roman society: in the Greek world, Constantine thoroughly Christianized the apparatus of the state. The fourth-century eastern empire was far more of a 'Christian empire' than the western. Yet paganism survived in the cultural life of the eastern empire far longer than in the western: widely respected 'Hellenes' maintained the university life of Athens, of Alexandria and of innumerable smaller centres right up to the Arab conquest. In the Harran outside Edessa (Urfa, eastern Turkey), pagan country-gentlemen survived untouched into the tenth century. They had made their own the speculations and the grievances of the last age of Greek thought. An astonishing oasis of 'Hellenism', they worshipped a triad of Divine Minds called 'Socrates, Plato and Aristotle'; they believed that Constantine had been a leper, who had cunningly changed Christianity into an imitation of Roman polytheism; they were convinced that the rise of Christianity had spelt the end of Greek science.

These 'Hellenes' impress us because, though open to the spiritual turmoil of their age, they turned to the ancient methods to find a solution for contemporary anxieties. Their quiet faith in a continuously evolving tradition stemming from Plato was perhaps the most reassuring facet of Late Antique civilization. For many a classical and enlightened society has collapsed under the weight of its own traditionalism, leaving to its immediate successors only a memory of anxiety and nightmares. That this did not happen in the Roman empire is largely due to the revival of the 'Hellenes', and to their dialogue with a new upper-class intelligentsia of Christians.

Plotinus, though outstanding as a thinker, is typical of them all in his evolution. An Egyptian, born in a small provincial town about 205, he had more than dabbled in Gnosticism. He had had the same teacher as the Christian Origen. He had attempted to find out about the exotic philosophy of the Persians and the Indians. Only later in life did he sink, with growing tranquillity, into the ancient dialectic of Plato. His writings have the appeal of a troubled and urgent man who has won his way by harsh, rational discipline to sweetness and clarity in his middle age. His pupils would still ask him the desperate questions of the previous generation: why is it that the soul has become united to this body? But Plotinus would give them no ready-made answers: he would insist on thrashing the matter out, 'in the Hellenic manner' – by days of dialectical inquiry sustained by the writings of Plato.

His followers, likewise, manned the religious frontier of their age. Porphyry of Tyre (*c.* 232–*c.* 303) wrote a prodigiously learned and devastating criticism of the Christian Scriptures: his critical remarks were not surpassed until the Higher Criticism of the nineteenth century. Porphyry's younger colleague, Iamblichus of Apamea (died *c.* 330), taught a whole generation of Greek youth. Like many professors, then as now, he readily posed as a mystagogue; he has the infuriating glibness of a popular teacher disposing of the crude imputations of the anti-religious. But at a time when Constantine was grouping a Christian court round himself, Iamblichus was able to reassure a whole generation of Greek gentlemen that their traditional beliefs were perfectly compatible with the most elevated Platonism. He had his revenge on Constantine. The last representative of Constantine's family, his gifted nephew Julian, was converted from Christianity back to 'Hellenism' by the pupils of Iamblichus. From 361 to 363, Julian 'the Apostate' reigned as emperor (see pp. 91–94). And even a century and a half after the battle for the public faith of the empire was lost to Christianity, the philosopher Proclus would be writing, in the mood of a still evening after thunder, intimate hymns to the gods and a totally pagan *Elements of Theology*.

The 'Hellenes' created the classical language of philosophy in the early Middle Ages, of which Christian, Jewish and Islamic thought, up to the twelfth century, are but derivative vernaculars. When the humanists of the Renaissance rediscovered Plato, what caught their enthusiasm was not the Plato of the modern classical scholar, but the living Plato of the religious thinkers of Late Antiquity.

Briefly, they believed that in Plato and in the intellectual discipline of the Greek universities, they had found a way of holding tensions, of maintaining both poles of a taut line, while the more radical thinkers and the more revolutionary movements round them had somehow allowed the line to snap. What they emphasized was that

73

it was possible, through rational contemplation, to seize the intimate connection between every level of the visible world and its source in the One God. It was possible, therefore, to 'touch' by thought the concentrated centre that had been sensed through the unrolled beauty of all visible things. To use a simple image, they viewed the world and its relation to God like a yo-yo rapidly spinning up and down on a thread. To them, the Gnostic had cut this thread: for the Gnostic said that there was no connection between the universe and a good God, between a man's inside and his outside, between his body and his soul. The Christian, by contrast, had not allowed the yo-yo to spin out: he had riveted his attention on the One God; the glare of the crude monotheism of the Christians drained away the rainbow articulations of invisible and visible gods, by which it was necessary that the beauty of the One should pass to mortal eyes.

To have upheld the connection between the visible and the invisible, between an inexpressible inner world and its meaningful articulation in the outside world, to maintain that it was possible for natural things to be charged with significance by the soul – this was the service which Plotinus rendered to his contemporaries and successors. Christians whose thought dominated the Middle Ages, St Augustine in the West and the unknown author of the *Celestial Hierarchies* (later known as 'Pseudo-Dionysius') who wrote about AD 500 in the East, were equally indebted to the passionately maintained equipoise of Plotinus.

To a Platonist, the relation between body and soul was a microcosm of the vexed problem of the relation between God and the universe. Plotinus' answer to this problem was characteristic. To have a body, he decided, was no more a 'sin' than for a man to cast a shadow. The body, indeed, was a beautiful instrument by which the soul sought expression: a man must cherish and train his body, as a musician must keep his lyre in tune. This is a taut, sensitive ideal, but totally unascetic. We can see what Plotinus meant if we look at the art that was being patronized by the generation that listened to him. This art is not 'otherworldly': it is 'innerworldly'. Far from abandoning the grace and individuality of the body, the portraits of the later empire gather up this body round the doors by which one can pass straight from the body into a man's mind. Their emphasis is on the eyes. The eyes flash out at us, revealing an inner life hidden in a charged cloud of flesh. Late Antiquity is an age of gripping portraits.

51 The power of the eyes. Homeric heroes disputing, from a sixth-century illustration of the *Iliad*: they speak to each other with their eyes, which, in contemporary icons, turn outwards to speak directly to the worshipper.

Not surprisingly, a Late Antique man produced the first, and one of the greatest, 'self-portraits': in the autobiographical *Confessions* of St Augustine, written in 397, the most brilliant Latin reader of Plotinus transmuted the impersonal intellectual passion of the Old Master into the first true 'self-portrait' of European literature.

Plotinus and Augustine represent one stream in the Platonic revival of Late Antiquity – the one that comes closest to modern men. Yet for contemporaries, and for men up to the seventeenth century, an equally important feature of Platonism was its attitude to man's place in the universe as a whole. In the writings of the 'Hellenes', men recaptured a lost sense of intimacy with the world around them.

Black Gnostic speculations, Christian monotheism, later Christian asceticism, threatened to leave a man lonely in a world drained of meaning. To the Late Antique philosophers, the world had, admittedly, become mysterious. They contemplated its beauty with sad thoughts, like the last fragile evening-glow of a long-set sun. But this universe, though mysterious, was meaningful: it was a sign from God. The inherited myths could be welcomed by the philosopher as signs (much as if the modern nuclear physicists had inherited from the past – instead of making them for themselves –

AN AGE OF PORTRAITS

52 The portrait developed in the third and fourth centuries to include intimate mementoes of a friend: (*left*) Eusebius, 'the sweet soul'. Fourth-century gold-leaf glass.

55, 56 (*right*) Philosophers from Aquileia and Athens: grave, hieratic images of the 'spiritual man'.

53, 54 The emperor Decius and the philosopher Dogmatius: tense and realistic treatment of public men in the Roman manner.

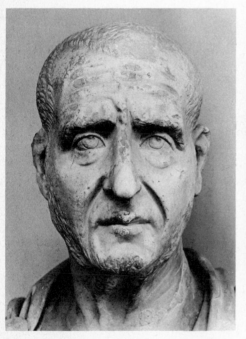

those naïve, two-dimensional sketches of the orbits of neutrons and protons that sum up, for the layman, vertiginous truths about the physical universe). Against the emptiness of the Christians' 'spiritual worship' in their cold basilicas, the pagan philosophers upheld the 'gestures charged with soul' of traditional sacrifice, as the burning altar reduced its offering to the simple clarity of rising flame.

The yearning for intimacy in a bottomless universe is expressed in the repetition of terms by which the Neoplatonic philosophers expressed the closeness of the One God to the infinite articulations of the visible world: they emphasized the 'chain' of beings, the 'inter-weaving', the 'intermingling', that linked man to his awesome source. All creatures responded to this unseen centre, as the lotus-flower quietly opens to the climbing sun.

In the fourth century such ideas were regarded as the crowning achievement and the sole hope of all civilized thinkers in the Roman empire. Christians shared them, inasmuch as they considered themselves to be civilized men. In the West, where intellectual life was spasmodic and lacked the firm bulwarks of a predominantly pagan university *milieu*, Christian intellectuals became the almost unchallenged heirs of Plotinus: the Christians, Marius Victorinus in the mid-fourth century, Ambrose, Augustine, later Boethius (*c.* 480–524), 77 were the bridgeheads between Greek philosophy and the Latin Middle Ages. Even in the East, pagan professors found themselves giving as generously to Christians as to their own: a typical quiet evolution from the schoolrooms of the philosophers into a bishopric was experienced by Synesius, bishop of Ptolemais from 410 to 414. Synesius could remain the friend of the pagan lady, Hypatia of Alexandria (see p. 104). He became bishop in 410, on condition that, while he might 'speak in myths' in church, he should be free to 'think as a philosopher' in private.

It is precisely the element in the revived Platonism which saved men from desolation and meaninglessness in the face of the visible world, that the Christians took over from their pagan masters. The world that had threatened, in the second and third centuries, to grow pale in the harsh light of the Christian Apologists' call to the simple worship of a half-known high God, became suffused again with colour. Augustine was delivered from Manichaeism, a Gnostic doctrine similar to those under whose shadow Plotinus had begun his intellectual odyssey, by reading Plotinus' *On Beauty*. Greek theologians found themselves debating the role and nature of Christ as He had appeared to men, against a classical backdrop of Platonic thought on the relation between God and the visible world. The 'interweaving' of human and divine by visible symbols, that so fascinated Iamblichus, is also a basic preoccupation of his younger contemporary, St Athanasius, when he writes on the Incarnation of Christ. The echo of divine beauty which had been rendered visible and so mysteriously potent, by the material image of a pagan god, later conveyed the same powers to the Christian icon. The paintings that cover the walls of a Byzantine church: the human saints that meet the believer at eye-level below scenes of the life of the Incarnate Christ; the tall Archangels who link Christ the Ruler of the Visible Universe, whose distant face merges against the gold of the highest vault, with the pictures that stride down the walls into the crowd below: this scheme of ascending figures is a direct echo of the awesome sense of an invisible world made visible by art, to souls caught in the veils of a body, that had once stirred in the emperor Julian, as he stood before the altar of his gods.

It was the sense of the intimate and intangible presence of the unseen that consoled the last pagans. To claim, as Christian mobs would claim in the late fourth century (see p. 104), that they had

57 The new pagan idiom. 'Our Lady of Many Blessings' on a sixth-century Egyptian tapestry. A majestic abstract figure, distributing the blessing of virtue and improvement, replaces the all too human gods of popular mythology.

'destroyed' the gods by destroying their temples, was as stupid for the pagan as to claim to have banished electricity by destroying all plugs and switches. The beautiful classical statues of the gods had been destroyed: but, said Julian, the Athenians had long ago destroyed the 'living statue' of the body of Socrates – his soul lived on. It was the same with the gods. In the stars at night, the gods had found shapes more suitable to their impassive eternity than perishable human statues. For, in the stars, the diffracted colours of earth were concentrated into a steady, imperturbable glow. The stars and the planets

58, 59 In a late medieval manuscript, the gods are shown in the planets, each circumscribed by its orbit (*Vat. Pal. Lat.* 1370).

swung safely above the heads of the last pagans, glittering statues of the gods far removed from the vandalism of the monks. Throughout the Middle Ages, the stars still hung above Christian Europe, disquieting reminders of the immortality of the gods. The gods had left their names on the days of the week. Their attributes still rested on the planets; and these planets ruled the behaviour of civilized men up to the end of the seventeenth century. After thirteen hundred years, men would still be recapturing, in more or less Christian form, that thrill of kinship with a perfect and inviolable world that had once turned the young Julian from Christianity.

> Sit, Jessica: look, how the floor of heaven
> Is thick inlaid with patines of bright gold:
> There's not the smallest orb which thou behold'st
> But in his motion like an angel sings,
> Still quiring to the young-eyed cherubins;
> Such harmony is in immortal souls;
> But, whilst this muddy vesture of decay
> Doth grossly close it in, we cannot hear it.

> (*Merchant of Venice*, Act v, scene i, 58–65)

60 Mercury still presides over the same professions and skills as are ascribed to this god in Late Antique literature: as the 'Thrice-Great Hermes', Mercury was regarded by pagans as the revealer of all art and culture. From a series of Florentine engravings, *The Planets*, 1464–65.

MERCVRIO
MERCVRIO E PIANETO MASCHVLINO POSTO NELSECONDO CIELO ET SECHO MAPERCHE LA
SVA SICITA EMOLTO PASSIVA LVI EFREDO CONQVEGLI SENGNI CH SONO FREDDI EVMIDO COG
LI VMIDI ELOQVENTE INGENGNIOSO AMA LESCIENSIE MATEMATICA ESTIVDIA NELLEDIVI
NASIONE A ILCORPO GRACILE COE SCHIETTO ELBRI SOTTILI ISTATVRA CHONPIVTA DE
METALLI A LARGIENTO VIVO ELDI SVO E MERCOLEDI COLLA PRIMA ORA 8 15 EZZ
LANOTTE SVA EDELDI DELLADOMENICHA A PERAMICO ILSOLE PER NIMICO AVENE
RE LASVA VITAOVERO ESALTATIONE EVIRGO LASV MORTE OVERO NVMILIASIONE
EPISCE HA HABITASIONE GEMNI DIDI VIRGO DINOTTE VA E IZ SENGNI IN
DI COMINCIANDO DA VIRGO IN ZO DI E Z ORE VA VN SENGNO

'If all men wanted to be Christians,' the pagan Celsus wrote in 168, 'the Christians would no longer want them.' By 300 this situation had changed entirely. Christianity had put down firm roots in all the great cities of the Mediterranean: in Antioch and Alexandria the Church had become probably the biggest, certainly the best-organized single religious group in the town. The Christian gains had been made in just that part of the Roman world that had emerged comparatively unscathed from the troubles of the late third century. Silence descended on the stoutly pagan provinces of the West. By contrast, Syria and Asia Minor, with their vocal Christian elements, stood out more sharply than ever before as provinces of undimmed prosperity and intellectual ferment.

The most decisive change of that time, however, cannot be reduced to a matter of the size of the Christian communities. It was more significant for the immediate future of Christianity that the leaders of the Christian Church, especially in the Greek world, found that they could identify themselves with the culture, outlook and needs of the average well-to-do civilian. From being a sect ranged against or to one side of Roman civilization, Christianity had become a church prepared to absorb a whole society. This is probably the most important *aggiornamento* in the history of the Church: it was certainly the most decisive single event in the culture of the third century. For the conversion of a Roman emperor to Christianity, of Constantine in 312, might not have happened – or, if it had, it would have taken on a totally different meaning – if it had not been preceded, for two generations, by the conversion of Christianity to the culture and ideals of the Roman world.

Origen of Alexandria (*c.* 185–*c.* 254) was the towering genius whose works summed up the possibility of such a venture in assimilation. His work, continued by a succession of Greek bishops, culminated in the writings of a contemporary and adviser of the emperor Constantine, Eusebius, bishop of Caesarea, from about 315 to about 340. For Origen and his disciples, Christianity was the 'natural', the 'original' religion. The 'seeds' of Christian doctrine had been sown by Christ in every man. Ever since the Creation they had been variously tended by Him. Christ, therefore, had 'tended' the best in Greek culture – especially Greek philosophy and ethics – as deliberately as He had revealed the Law to the Jews; the foundation

82

61 'A mighty soul, who acted on the prompting of God.' The raised eyes in this colossal head of Constantine, now outside the Palazzo dei Conservatori, Rome, emphasize the emperor's idea of himself as a man in close contact with God.

of the universal Christian Church by Christ had been expressly synchronized with the foundation of a universal Roman peace by Augustus. A Christian, therefore, could reject neither Greek culture nor the Roman empire without seeming to turn his back on part of the divinely ordained progress of the human race. Christ was the 'schoolmaster' of the human race, and Christianity was the peak of His education, the 'true' *paideia*, the 'true' culture. Origen and his successors taught the pagan that to become a Christian was to step, at last, from a confused and undeveloped stage of moral and intellectual growth into the heart of civilization. On the sarcophagi and frescoes of the late third century, Christ appears as the Divine Schoolmaster, dressed in the simple robes of a professor of literature, lecturing – as Origen must have done – to a quiet circle of well-groomed disciples. The Christian bishop had become part of the intelligentsia of many a great Greek town: he, also, sat on a professor's 'chair' – his *cathedra*; and he was thought of as 'lecturing' his *didaskaleion*, his study-group, on simple and elevating ethical themes.

The early fourth century was the great age of the Christian Apologists – Lactantius (*c.* 240–*c.* 320), writing in Latin, and Eusebius of Caesarea, in Greek. Their appeals to the educated public coincided with the last, the 'Great Persecution of the Church', from 302 to 310, and with the conversion and reign of Constantine as a Christian emperor from 312 to 337. The Christianity of the Apologists was not merely a religion that had found a *modus vivendi* with the civilization that surrounded it. They presented it as something far more than that. They claimed that Christianity was the sole guarantee of that civilization – that the best traditions of classical philosophy and the high standards of classical ethics could be steeled against barbarism only through being confirmed by the Christian revelation; and that the beleaguered Roman empire was saved from destruction only by the protection of the Christian God.

Such a message played on the 'Great Fear' of the townsmen of the Mediterranean world of the late third century. One should always remember that classical civilization was the civilization of a fragile veneer: only one man in ten lived in the civilized towns. At no time did this urban crust feel its hold over a wide world to be more precarious than at the end of the third century. The townsmen had maintained their privileges. But they were dwarfed by a countryside whose face had become less recognizable to classical men. In many rural areas, from Britain to Syria, archaic cults, far removed from the classical Olympians, reared their heads more insistently than ever before. The primitive tribes from beyond the frontiers had made their presence felt in terrifying *razzias*. Furthermore, the traditional protectors of the towns, the emperors and their army, had never seemed so alien. The Roman army was stationed among, and recruited from, the populations of the frontiers. It had always been an outsider in the Mediterranean world: in the generation before the accession of Diocletian, in 284, it was in danger of becoming a foreign body. The Danubian provincials who saved the empire needed to be told by their commanders that they did so to preserve, not to terrorize, the civilians. When we compare the rough, uniformed figures of Diocletian and his colleagues with the exquisitely classical sarcophagi of contemporary upper-class Christians, we realize that, against the gulf which threatened to open between the new masters of the empire and the traditions of the ancient cities, the old division between pagan and Christian civilian might seem insignificant. By 300, the Christian

62 Christ the teacher. Fifth-century ivory pyxis.

bishop had at least become part of the landscape of most towns: in the civilized Greek world it was the Latin-speaking soldier who was the outsider.

With the return of peace after the accession of Diocletian, the wound began to close between the new, military governing class and the urban civilization of the Mediterranean. But there were now two groups who claimed to represent this civilization: the traditional pagan governing class, whose resilience and high standards had been shown in the revival and spread of Platonic philosophy in the late third century, were in danger of being outbid by the new, 'middle-brow' culture of the Christian bishops, whose organizing power and adaptability had been proved conclusively in the previous generation.

At first, organization for survival was more important to the emperors than culture. Diocletian was a sincere, *borné* Roman traditionalist; yet he ruled for nineteen years without giving a thought to the Christians. The 'Great Persecution', which began in 302 and continued spasmodically for a decade, came as a brutal shock to respectable Christians. They found themselves officially outcastes in the society with which they had so strenuously identified themselves. It was a terrifying and, on the whole, a deeply demoralizing experience. They were saved by an obscure event. In 312, a usurping emperor, Constantine, won a battle over his rival at the Milvian Bridge, outside Rome. He ascribed this victory to the protection of the Christian God, vouchsafed in a vision.

If God helps those who help themselves, then no group better deserved the miracle of the 'conversion' of Constantine in 312 than did the Christians. For the Christian leaders seized their opportunity with astonishing pertinacity and intelligence. They besieged Constantine in his new mood: provincial bishops, notably Hosius of Cordova (*c.* 257–357), attached themselves to his court; other bishops, from Africa, swept him into their local affairs as a judge; Lactantius emerged as tutor to his son; and, when Constantine finally conquered the eastern provinces in 324, he was greeted by Eusebius of Caesarea, who placed his pen at the emperor's disposal with a skill and enthusiasm such as no traditional Greek rhetor had seemed able to summon up for Constantine's grim and old-fashioned predecessors – Diocletian and Galerius.

This prolonged exposure to Christian propaganda was the true

63 'It is the greatest crime to wish to undo what has been fixed and established by antiquity': Diocletian and his colleagues performing a pagan sacrifice. Christian courtiers had even attended on such occasions. During the Great Persecution, Christians were spasmodically forced to perform these sacrifices: for a pagan, they were a natural and graceful gesture to the gods (*cf.* Ill. 85). Detail from the Arch of Galerius, Salonica.

'conversion' of Constantine. It began on a modest scale when he controlled only the under-Christianized western provinces; but it reached its peak after 324, when the densely Christianized territories of Asia Minor were united to his empire. Its results were decisive. Constantine could easily have been merely a 'god-fearing' emperor, who, for reasons of his own, was prepared to tolerate the Christians: there had been many such in the third century (one of whom, Philip (244–49), was even regarded as a crypto-Christian). Given the religious climate of the age, there was no reason, either, why his decision to tolerate the Church might not have been ascribed to intimations from the Christian God. Constantine rejected this easy and obvious solution. He came to be the emperor we know from his speeches and edicts: a crowned Christian Apologist. He viewed himself and his mission as a Christian emperor in the light of the interpretation of Christianity that had been presented to the average educated layman by the Christian Apologists of his age. In becoming a Christian, Constantine publicly claimed to be saving the Roman empire; even more – in mixing with bishops, this middle-aged Latin soldier sincerely believed that he had entered the charmed circle of 'true' civilization, and had turned his back on the Philistinism of the raw men who had recently attacked the Church.

One suspects that Constantine was converted to many more aspects of Mediterranean life than to Christianity alone. The son of a soldier, he threw in his lot with a civilian way of life that had been largely ignored by the grey administrators of the age of Diocletian. From 311 onwards, Constantine put the landed aristocracy on its feet again: he is the 'restorer of the Senate', to whom the aristocracy of the West owed so much. In 332, he gave these landowners extensive powers over their tenants. After 324, he grouped a new civilian governing class round himself in the Greek East (see p. 27). He gave the provincial gentry of Asia Minor what they had long wanted: Constantinople, a 'new' Rome, placed within convenient range of the imperial court as it moved along the routes connecting the Danube to Asia Minor. For the Greek senator and bureaucrat, roads that had long ceased to lead to Rome converged quite naturally at this new capital.

Constantine, very wisely, seldom said 'no'. The first Christian emperor accepted pagan honours from the citizens of Athens. He ransacked the Aegean for pagan classical statuary to adorn Constantinople. He treated a pagan philosopher as a colleague. He paid the travelling expenses of a pagan priest who visited the pagan monuments of Egypt. After a generation of 'austerity' for everyone, and of 'terror' for the Christians, Constantine, with calculated flamboyance, instituted the 'Great Thaw' of the early fourth century: it was a whole restored civilian world, pagan as well as Christian, that was pressing in round the emperor.

In this restored world, the Christians had the advantage of being the most flexible and open group. The bishops could accept an uncultivated emperor. They were used to autodidacts, to men of genuine eccentric talent who – so they claimed – were taught by God alone. Constantine, one should remember, was the younger contemporary of the first Christian hermit, St Anthony (see p. 96). Neither the Latin-speaking soldier nor the Coptic-speaking farmer's son would have been regarded as acceptable human material for a classical schoolmaster: yet Eusebius of Caesarea wrote the life of Constantine the soldier, and Athanasius of Alexandria – an equally sophisticated Greek – the life of Anthony the Egyptian. It was over the wide bridge of a 'middlebrow' identification of Christianity with a lowest com-

64 Constantius II (337–61), son of Constantine. Very much a Byzantine autocrat, he entered Rome, standing as immobile as a statue, 'looking neither to right nor left, as if his head were held in a vice'. Fourth-century bronze head.

mon denominator of classical culture, and not through the narrow gate of a pagan aristocracy of letters, that Constantine and his successors entered the civilian civilization of the Mediterranean.

The reign of his son, Constantius II, from 337 to 361, set the seal on the new style of life. This limited and much-maligned man turned his father Constantine's sleight of hand into a lasting reality. The bishops joined the bureaucrats as members of the new governing class that was centred on the emperor's court. Constantine had already made his most amiable (and enigmatic) claims to be a 'bishop extraordinary' of the Christian Church in the mellow atmosphere of an imperial dinner-party. Under Constantius II, however, the bishops learnt that, if they were courtiers, they must be prepared to rise and fall like courtiers: Athanasius of Alexandria was exiled five times (seventeen and a half years of his life); the bishop of Antioch was denounced for libelling the empress and was framed with prostitutes; these are the ugly symptoms of the formation of yet another privileged group on the fringes of the mighty palace.

89

The religious policy of Constantius II showed his characteristically shrewd pursuit of a middle way. He upheld Arianism, as being the more philosophically acceptable statement of the relation between Christ and God the Father. This creed was formulated by an Alexandrian priest, Arius (*c.* 250–*c.* 336), in the face of the intransigent hostility of his ecclesiastical superior, the authoritarian Athanasius, patriarch of Alexandria. Arius enjoyed the tacit support of cultivated bishops, such as the elder statesman, Eusebius of Caesarea. In supporting Arianism, Constantius opted for the religion of the cultivated Christian Apologists of a previous generation, against the suspect new piety of Athanasius, based on the mounting enthusiasm of the Egyptian monks. As seen by the average bishop of the age of Constantine, the victory of Christianity had been a victory of strict monotheism over polytheism. The martyrs had died for a single, high God. And for the cultivated Christian of the fourth century, a high God could only manifest Himself to the physical universe through an intermediary. Christ had to be, in some way, a reflection of God; He could not possibly *be* God: for the lonely essence of the One God must stand concentrated and transcendent. The God of the Arians was the jealous God of Abraham, of Isaac and of Jacob: but their Christ was the godlike intermediary of the high-pitched universe of the Neoplatonic philosophers. Arianism also appealed to the imagination of a new court society. For Christ was thought of as 'representing' God in this world, much as a governor, sitting beneath an icon of the emperor, 'represented' Constantius II in a distant court-house.

Constantius II enjoyed the support of the well-educated and traditionally minded bishops of Asia Minor and of the Danubian provinces. It is a grouping of parties that foreshadows the frontiers of the medieval Byzantine empire: a solid bloc of conservative, loyalist 'Romans' of predominantly Greek culture was already holding the balance between a primitive Latin West, and an exuberant East. The secular counterparts of these bishops flocked to Constantinople: they brought the language and the building-styles of Greek Asia Minor into the new capital. Both laymen and bishops were groomed in Greek culture: they had read their Homer and some had even been to Athens. But their classicism was the 'pasteurized' success-culture of the early fourth century (see p. 30); they read Greek literature to gain the skills of a gentleman, not to learn about the gods.

65 Julian the Apostate (361–63). After a succession of close-shaven Latin autocrats, Julian flaunted the long beard of a Greek philosopher.

Such men deserved the sudden fright of nineteen months of ostentatiously pagan rule – the reign of the emperor Julian the Apostate, from 361 to 363.

By a chance of fortune, Julian, a nephew of Constantine, had found himself free to gain a proper education. While his older cousin, Constantius II, patrolled the empire with his *déraciné* court, Julian 'went native' among the educated Greeks of the Aegean cities (see p. 70). He was swept to the throne by a desperate Gallic army: but he ruled as the first emperor of genuine education for a century, and as an emperor more austere and articulate than Marcus Aurelius.

Julian spoke up for the 'community of the Hellenes'. He represented the depressed gentry of the ancient Greek towns of Asia Minor – 'honest men' who had watched with growing anger the blasphemies, the indecent affluence, the deep intellectual confusion of the court society of Constantine and Constantius II. By instituting lavish pagan ceremonies and by increasing the status of pagan priests, Julian

66 A religion of the book. The four neat *codices* of the Evangelists stand in a cupboard (very different from the elaborate ancient scrolls in Ill. 23). Fifth-century mosaic in the Mausoleum of Galla Placidia, Ravenna.

showed them that the gods existed and could be seen to exist. He established a régime of 'austerity', after the mushroom growth of court life since Constantine. He reminded the upper classes of landmarks that had been washed away by the social fluidity of the early fourth century: he urged them to remember the ancient status of the pagan priesthoods, and the old traditions of social responsibility for the poor. He wished to reunite, round their ancient temples, towns that had fallen apart between *nouveaux riches* and depressed gentry, between town council and Christian bishop.

This 'pagan reaction' of Julian's reign was far from being a romantic effort to put the clock back to the days of Marcus Aurelius. Like so many 'reactions', it was an angry attempt to settle scores with collaborators. Julian was naturally disturbed by the rapid spread of Christianity among the lower classes; but the real objects of his hatred were those members of the Greek upper classes who had compromised with the Christianity of the régimes of Constantine and Constantius II. It was the *demi-vierge* classicism of upper-class

Christians that he attacked with such vigour. *Paideia*, classical culture, he insisted, was the gift of the gods to men. The Christians had abused the heaven-sent gift of Greek culture: their Apologists had used Greek erudition and philosophical questionings to blaspheme the gods; Christian courtiers had battened on Greek literature to appear civilized. In 363, Christians were forbidden to teach Greek literature: 'If they want to learn literature, they have Luke and Mark: let them go back to their churches and expound them.'

Julian died on an expedition to Persia at the age of thirty-one, in 363. Had he lived, he intended that Christianity should sink out of the governing classes of the empire – much as Buddhism was driven back into the lower classes by a revived Confucian mandarinate in thirteenth-century China. Whatever the 'barbarian' ramifications of Christianity in the lower classes, the 'mandarins' of Julian's Roman empire were to be authentic 'Hellenes' – men reared on Homer, and impermeable to the gospels of Galilean fishermen. It is a measure of the shrewdness of Julian's diagnosis of the resources of Hellenism in the later empire, that many Greeks – as professors, poets, *littérateurs* and administrators – managed to be staunch 'Hellenic' pagans up to the end of the sixth century.

Seldom have the issues of half a century been summed up so clearly and judged so trenchantly as in the writings and policies of Julian the Apostate. Yet Julian was proved wrong. The fact that his works were preserved at all for posterity proves that a compromise between Christianity and Hellenism had come to stay: for the writings of the Apostate are preserved for us in *de luxe* editions, lovingly produced by humanist monks and bishops in thirteenth-century Byzantium.

It was not that Julian was unrealistic. He saw, with a clarity bred of hatred, one blatant feature of his age – Christianity rising like a damp-stain up the wall of his beloved Hellenic culture. What he did not see was that this same Christianity was able to pass the classical culture of an élite to the average citizen of the Roman world. The Christian bishops were the missionaries of the culture with which they had identified themselves.

For Christianity was an essentially 'Cockney' religion. It had clung to the contours of urban life throughout the empire. It was 'Cockney', also, in assuming at least a minimal participation in literacy: the first thing an Egyptian peasant found himself being made to do, on joining a monastery, was learning to read – so as to understand the

Bible. (The establishment of Christianity coincided, significantly, with a notable advance in book-production, by which the clumsy scroll was replaced by the compact *codex*, like the modern book with opening pages.)

To take some local examples: to Julian, 'Hellenism' seemed a fragile veneer in a backward province such as Cappadocia. The Christian bishops of the Cappadocian cities, however, though of the same class as their pagan colleagues, were less deterred by the intractable 'barbarism' of the surrounding population. They resolutely preached at them in Greek, recruited them into Greek-speaking monasteries, and sent Greek-speaking priests out to them in the countryside. As a result, Cappadocia became a Greek-speaking province up to the fourteenth century.

The flexible, doctrinaire Greek of the bishop could travel faster than the patient, inward-looking classicism of the rhetor. It could be translated and transposed even beyond the frontiers of the empire. From the fourth century onwards Armenia became a sub-Byzantine province through its ecclesiastical links with Cappadocia: even the vowel-sounds of Armenian transliterations preserve a classical Greek pronunciation that has long vanished in Greece itself. Whenever we say 'church' we echo the Cappadocian Christians who influenced the translation of the Bible into Gothic: for the Gothic *ciric* (hence our 'church', *kerk*, *Kirche*) is derived from the *kyriakos oikos* – 'the Lord's house' – of Christian Greek.

In Egypt, also, Christianity fostered the growth of Coptic as a literary language. The adoption of Coptic is by no means a sign of a resurgence of Egyptian 'separatism', as has often been confidently asserted. In the fourth and fifth centuries, Egyptian 'isolationism' was pagan. It concentrated on the 'holy land' of Egypt and its temples, and it expressed itself in Greek. Coptic, by contrast, was a literature of participation. It abounded in loan-words; and, through Coptic, the clergy and monks of Upper Egypt felt that, for the first time in their immemorial history, they could embrace distant thoughts and policies, and could set the tone of a common monastic culture, as far away as Constantinople and Gaul. Just as the Danubian provincial had shown that, through the army, he could gain a stake in the Roman empire without flaunting a knowledge of the classics, so the Christian Egyptian, Syrian, or North African now felt involved in the religious issues that preoccupied the governing class of the empire.

94

67 The new Christian participant: Rhodia, from the Fayum, Egypt. Sixth-century tombstone.

When Plotinus was unravelling the wisdom of Plato in a senator's villa outside Rome (from 244 to 270), far away, in Plotinus' home-country, Egypt, the son of a family of well-to-do peasants was attending the Christian church in his village. This young man, Anthony, took the saying of Jesus that was read out in the lesson – 'Go, sell all you have and give to the poor and follow me' – as a command addressed to himself. He began to lead the life of a hermit in about 269. Gradually, he weaned himself from the outskirts of his village, and struck out further and further into the Outer Desert, in 285. When he died in 356, at the age of 105, he had lived for over seventy years in a forbidding wilderness, some weeks' journey from the nearest town. Anthony had dropped out of civilization as ancient man had known it. Yet Anthony became the 'father of the monks'. He was the hero of a masterly biography by none other than Athanasius, the patriarch of Alexandria. The shy son of Egyptian farmers, who had avoided going to school, came to influence the Christian Church in every town of the Roman empire.

These two remarkable Egyptians – Plotinus and Anthony – mark the parting of the ways in the religious history of Late Antiquity. They shared in a common climate of opinion: Plotinus 'lived as one ashamed to have been born into a human body', and Anthony 'blushed' when he had to eat. Both men were admired for having achieved a 'godlike' mastery of mind over body. But the means they had chosen to the same end were diametrically opposed. For Plotinus and his pagan successors, otherworldliness rose out of the traditional culture, like the last icy peak of a mountain range: a training in classical literature and philosophy stood at the base of the asceticism of the late Roman philosopher, as seemingly irremovable as the foothills of the Himalayas. The 'godlike' man of paganism could only be produced from among intellectuals who had undergone the ancient grooming in the ways of a civilized gentleman. As we have seen, the average Christian bishop of the late third and early fourth centuries had come very close to sharing this ideal – austere, highly literate, exclusively urban. But the Christian Church had remained open to other forms of talent: even the learned Origen, for instance, had left room in the Christian Church for the 'simple' folk who would take the commands of Christ literally. Within a generation of the time of

68 The monk, his hands lifted in prayer. Coptic limestone relief, sixth–seventh century.

Origen, Christianity had begun to spread into the villages of Egypt, of Syria and (to a lesser extent) of North Africa. Men like Anthony would be listening to the radical sayings of Christ, and, like Anthony, they reacted drastically, by making a total break with their environment. The break is summed up in a term long used of villagers in Egypt who had opted out in moments of distress or oppression – *anachoresis* (hence our 'anchorite'): becoming a 'displaced person'.

For Plotinus and many a Christian bishop, disengagement from the world was quietly distilled without any break with the surrounding culture and society. An explicit, physical gesture of 'displacement' lay at the root of the spiritual life of Anthony: to leave the civilized world was the necessary first step in the new ascetic movement. In whatever way he might show it, the new Christian holy man had opted for some flagrant antithesis to the norms of civilized life in the Mediterranean. Inevitably, therefore, the way such men organized themselves, the culture they created, the standards of behaviour they preached, even the places where they preferred to congregate, marked a break with what had gone before. The appeal and significance of the asceticism that swept the Roman world in the fourth century lies precisely in this: it was a grouping of self-styled 'displaced persons', who claimed to have started life afresh.

This Christian 'displacement' spread with astonishing rapidity from many areas. Mesopotamia was the centre of one such explosion, whose shock waves rippled across the Near East. The Syrian asceticism of the area round Nisibis and Edessa, especially the forbidding mountains of Tur 'Abdin (the mountains of the 'Servants of God', i.e. the monks), spread northwards into Armenia, and westwards to the streets of Antioch: it enriched and troubled the life of Mediterranean cities as far apart as Constantinople, Milan and Carthage.

The Syrians were the 'stars' of the ascetic movement: wild vagrants dressed in skins, their matted hair making them look like eagles, these 'men of fire' amazed and disquieted the Greco-Roman world by their histrionic gestures. Their most typical representatives, in the fifth century, were the 'Stylite' saints – men who squatted on the top of pillars. The founder of this idiosyncrasy, Simeon (*c.* 396–459), held court for forty years from the top of a fifty-foot column in the mountainous hinterland of Antioch.

In Egypt, by contrast, asceticism took a different turn. A canny and anxious peasantry steered clear of the ferocious individualism of the

69 The 'star'. St Simeon Stylites (from the Greek *stylos*, a pillar) squatting on his pillar. He had outfaced the devil as a great snake. Clients would consult him by climbing up the ladder (on the left). Mementoes such as this one – the first Christian icons – spread the fame of Simeon as far apart as Persia, Rome and Paris. Gold plaque from a sixth-century Syrian reliquary.

Syrians. The Egyptians felt that they lived in a confusing world, laid like a minefield with the snares of the devil, and all too easily disrupted by the full-blooded quarrelsomeness of their fellow villagers turned monks. They opted for humility, for a limited but relentless routine of prayer and manual labour, for safety in numbers, for an iron discipline. Pachomius (*c.* 290–347), a farmer once press-ganged into the army of Constantine, set about creating an organized monastic life, linking the cells of the hermits into great settlements in Upper Egypt – beginning at Tabennisi in the Thebaid in 320. His 'colony' was conceived with an ingenuity, implemented with a discipline and expanded with a speed and flexibility that quite surpassed any of the organizational ventures of the late Roman state: by the end of the fourth century, the great monasteries conceived by Pachomius harboured seven thousand monks.

70 The *Apa*, father of the monks. The spiritual director could be an awesome figure of authority. 'The spirit of the Lord is with that man,' said a monk of St Pachomius, 'and if he says die I die, and if he says live I live.' Coptic basalt stele, probably an abbot's tombstone, sixth–seventh century.

71 Victory over the demons. St Sisinnios, a rider saint, transfixes a female demon. Sixth- or seventh-century Egyptian fresco, monastery of St Apollo, Bawit.

The Egyptian experiments created an ethos all of their own. The Egyptian 'fathers' – the *Apa* (hence our word 'abbot') – had provided models for monastic communities that were set up, in the late fourth century, as far apart as Caesarea in Cappadocia, and Rouen. Their *Sayings* provided a remarkable new literary genre, close to the world of parable and folk-wisdom, whose themes and anecdotes were passed on throughout the Middle Ages and far into pre-revolutionary Russia. In these *Sayings*, the peasantry of Egypt spoke for the first time to the civilized world. There is hardly a saint in medieval Europe whose temptations are not modelled on those first described in connection with Anthony on the outskirts of an Egyptian village.

We know very little about the origin of the ascetic movement in its Near Eastern background, but enough to suspect any simple answer. It has been said that monasticism was a movement of flight and of protest: that the oppressed peasantry fled to the safety of the great monasteries, and that their grievances against their landowners mingled with the fanaticism with which they attacked the classical paganism and classical culture of the Greek cities. In fact, the founders of the monastic movement and their recruits were not oppressed peasants. Their *malaise* was more subtle. Late Roman Egypt was a land of vigorous villages where tensions sprang quite as much from the disruptive effects of new wealth and new opportunities as from the immemorial depredations of the tax-collector. Egyptian and Syrian villages came to produce more well-to-do eccentrics, whose talents found no outlet in the prudent and rooted routines of successful peasant communities: Anthony was an educational misfit; Macarius had been a smuggler; Pachomius had been uprooted by military service; the amiable Moses had been a highwayman.

However little we may know of the origin of the ascetic movement, we know a lot about the function and meaning of the monk's act of 'displacement' in fourth- and fifth-century society. The holy man was thought to have gained freedom and a mysterious power, through having passed through the many visible boundaries of a society, that was not so much oppressed, as stubbornly organized for survival. In villages dedicated for millennia to holding their own against nature, the holy man had deliberately chosen 'anti-culture' – the neighbouring desert, the nearest mountain crags. In a civilization identified exclusively with town life, the monks had committed the absurd – they had 'made a city in the desert'. Above all, in a world where the human race was thought of as besieged by invisible demonic powers (see pp. 53 ff.), the monks earned their reputation through being 'prize-fighters' against the devil. They held his malevolence at bay; and they were able – as the average man, with all his amulets and remedies against sorcery, never felt able – to laugh the devil in the face. The holy man's powers were shown in his relations with the animal kingdom, which had always symbolized the savagery and destructiveness of the demons: he drove out snakes and birds of prey, and he would settle down as the benign master of jackals and lions. Above all, the holy man was thought to have arrived at the most enviable prerogative to which an inhabitant of the later empire could aspire: he had gained *parrhesia*, 'freedom to speak' before the awesome majesty of God. For the God of the fourth-century Christian was an emperor writ large. Only those of His subjects who had spent their lives in unquestioning and tremulous obedience to His commands might feel free to approach Him, as favoured courtiers, and so have their prayers answered with spectacular results.

It is in such a belief that we catch a vivid glimpse of the quality of the public life of the later empire as it impinged on the popular imagination. The later Roman empire was not a world of great dislocation and oppression, so much as of unremitting thoroughness; it was a world where the penal laws of God and of the emperors were brutally and relentlessly applied, and where hope lay, not in revolution or reform, but rather in occasional unexpected favours obtained by the unpredictable interventions of a powerful few. When a holy man died, his life would often be remembered in the locality as a fragile patch of sunshine breaking the harsh climate of normal life: for the holy man's influence at the court of Heaven had gained a momentary amnesty from the iron laws of God's stern dealings with the Mediterranean peasant – a halt to plagues, to famine, to earthquakes, to hailstorms.

And, if God was conceived of in this hard way in Heaven, on earth the emperor and his servants were dreaded in earnest. Once again, the holy man emerges as one of the only forces in east Roman society who could stand in the way of the emperor's justice. When the citizens of Antioch expected savage punishment after a riot in 387, the imperial commissioners suddenly found their way to the doomed city barred by a group of Syriac-speaking holy men. While these wild figures interceded for the city, and their speeches were translated from Syriac into Greek, the bystanders 'stood around', wrote a witness, 'and shivered'.

The idea of the holy man holding the demons at bay and bending the will of God by his prayers came to dominate Late Antique society. In many ways, the idea is as new as the society itself. For it placed a man, a 'man of power', in the centre of people's imagination. Previously, the classical world had tended to think of its religion in terms of *things*. Ancient religion had revolved round great temples, against whose ancient stones even the most impressive priest had paled into insignificance; the gods had spoken impersonally at their oracle-sites; their ceremonies assumed a life in which the community, the city, dwarfed the individual. In the fourth and fifth centuries, however, the individual, as a 'man of power', came to dwarf the traditional communities: the person of the emperor had eclipsed the Senate and the city of Rome; the rise to prominence of the single

72 The holy man as a friend of Christ. Just as Diocletian rested his hand on his colleague's shoulder (Ill. 12), so St Menas is designated by Christ as his trusted colleague and adviser. Sixth- or seventh-century painted panel from Bawit, Egypt.

patronus, the protector, threatened to erode the solidarity of the town council (see p. 37). Simeon the Stylite, gloriously conspicuous on his column, sifting lawsuits, prophesying, healing, rebuking and advising the governing classes of the whole eastern empire not far from the deserted temple of Baalbek, was the sign of a similar change. In the popular imagination, the emergence of the holy man at the expense of the temple marks the end of the classical world.

At the end of the fourth century, the temples of the gods had survived in most great cities and in the surrounding countryside. After Constantine, they were partly 'secularized'; but they continued to be visited, and they were respected as public monuments by cultivated townsmen, pagan and Christian alike, rather like the beautiful cathedrals of some Communist states. To many bishops, however, they were a source of 'infection' to their congregations. To the monks, they were the fortresses of their enemy, the devil. By the late fourth century, there were some two thousand monks within striking distance of the great temples of Alexandria. Among such men, a life of 103 harsh obedience and continuous effort to control one's thoughts and body had created an atmosphere of explosive aggression, directed against the Evil One and his surviving representatives on earth. From Mesopotamia to North Africa, a wave of religious violence swept town and countryside: in 388 the monks burnt a synagogue at Callinicum near the Euphrates; at the same time, they terrorized the village-temples of Syria; in 391, the patriarch of Alexandria, Theophilus, called them in to 'purge' the city of the great shrine of Serapis, the Serapeum. Bands of monastic vigilantes, led by Schenudi of Atripe (died *c.* 466), patrolled the towns of Upper Egypt, ransacking the houses of pagan notables for idols. In North Africa, similar wandering monks, the 'Circumcellions', armed with cudgels called 'Israels', stalked the great estates, their cry of 'Praise be to God' more fearful than the roaring of a mountain-lion. In 415, the Egyptian monks shocked educated opinion by lynching a noble Alexandrian lady, Hypatia.

Paganism, therefore, was brutally demolished from below. For the pagans, cowed by this unexpected wave of terrorism, it was the end of the world. 'If we are alive,' wrote one, 'then life itself is dead.'

Yet this atrocious interlude was part of a deeper change. In the last decades of the fourth century, Christianity asserted itself, for the first time, as the majority religion of the Roman empire. Mobilized by his bishops, the Christian man in the street had got what he wanted. The Christian congregations of the 380s wanted a 'Christian' empire, purged of the heavy legacy of the gods, and ruled by an emperor who shared their prejudices against Jews, heretics and pagans. The emperors gave them their head. It was a cunning move on their part, for the towns of the later empire were jungles, under-policed and constantly threatened by famine and rioting. In the later fourth century, these towns had to meet a sudden, increased strain of high taxation, due to the renewal of barbarian invasions in the Balkans. When the townspeople rioted on matters that directly affected the financial and military needs of the emperors, they were ruthlessly suppressed. In 390, the emperor Theodosius I (379–95) massacred the inhabitants of Thessalonica when they lynched their military governor; he nearly did the same to the people of Antioch, when they refused to pay taxes. Yet he congratulated the Christians of Alexandria for having taken the law into their own hands in destroying the Serapeum, one of the wonders of the ancient world. Firm government

73 Theophilus, patriarch of Alexandria. This fragment of a fifth-century Alexandrian chronicle shows him treading on the ruins of the Serapeum.

74 (*above right*) Ambrose, bishop of Milan. A provincial governor who became bishop, he ensured that the emperors disestablished official pagan worship in Rome, and he made Theodosius do penance for his sins. 'We priests', he wrote, 'have our own ways of rising to power.' Fifth-century mosaic from Sant'Ambrogio, Milan.

75 Theodosius the Great (379–95). From a silver *missorium* of the late fourth century.

76 The Christ of the last day is no longer the graceful beardless teacher, but an awesome world ruler. Mid fourth-century wall painting from the Catacomb of Commodilla, Rome.

77 The last judgment. Christ sits on his judge's throne (*cf.* Ill. 32), surrounded by his advisers the Apostles, who as protectors – *patroni* – put in a word for their clients standing below. A typically late Roman tribunal, Christ and his Apostles are shown cut off from the acclaiming crowd by a lattice-work railing, exactly as in the scenes on the Arch of Constantine (Ill. 27). Fourth-century Roman terracotta plaque.

was not enough. The city dwellers had to be wooed and pampered if they were to be kept quiet. The Roman empire had remained a 'commonwealth of cities'; and in this 'commonwealth of cities' the Christian bishop, now ruling large congregations and backed by the violence of the monks, had come to the fore. The emperor Theodosius committed the bloodbath of Thessalonica, his statues were overturned and pelted by the citizens of Antioch: yet he went down to history as Theodosius 'the Great', the exemplary Catholic monarch. He had allied himself with the 'grass-roots' movements of the great cities of the empire. At Milan, he bowed dutifully before the bishop, St Ambrose; at Rome, he worshipped at the shrine of St Peter and poured money into a magnificent new basilica to St Paul (S. Paolo fuori le Mura). At Alexandria, he condoned the atrocities of Theophilus. Like the duke of Plaza Toro, Theodosius the Great led his regiment from the rear: he and his court followed, with exceptional sensitivity, the seismic shift that had placed the Christian bishop and the holy man at the head of popular opinion in the nerve-centres of the empire.

The monks, of course, were never more than a tiny proportion of the population of the empire. Nevertheless, it was paradoxically just these eccentrics who turned Christianity into a mass religion. They did this largely through their ability to sum up, in their persons, the piety of the average Roman now turned Christian. This was very different from the inward-looking devotion of previous centuries. In the third century, the Christian Church had been a tiny community of 'initiates'. Those who had passed through the 'mystery' of baptism were already among the 'saved'. By the late fourth century, it was far less certain that the masses who had passed through a perfunctory baptism in this world would be saved in the next. Men's anxieties, therefore, shifted to a more distant event: to the drastic settling of accounts at the Last Judgment. The earlier imagery of the afterlife, which showed a quiet group of initiates enjoying their sheltered idyll in another world – resting in the cool glow of the stars or in the shade of an arbour – gave place to the awesome thought of Christ as Emperor and Judge, before Whose throne the population of the whole Roman world must one day stand.

Like a lightning flash from a charged cloud, the ascetic movement exploded among populations increasingly preoccupied by this new, basic anxiety: it is no coincidence that the earliest monks were recruited in just those areas of the Roman world where Christianity had already been widespread for a long time. In living a life of prolonged anxiety and self-denial, the monk was admired for his ability to forestall the terrors of the Last Judgment by having taken them on himself in this life. His drastic example spurred on the Christian layman to prepare as best he could for the final *cause célèbre* between himself and God. In theory at least, the Christianized Roman empire of the fifth century onwards, was pervaded by the tense and purposeful mood of the antechamber of a court-house.

Hence a further paradox, by which precisely those bishops who were most affected by the 'otherworldly' preoccupations of the ascetic movement were those who did most to establish the Christian Church in Roman society. The amazing generation of ecclesiastical rulers at the end of the fourth and early fifth centuries – Ambrose at Milan (374–97), Basil at Caesarea (370–79), John Chrysostom at Antioch and Constantinople (398–407), Augustine at Hippo (391–430) – firmly believed that they would have to stand before Christ in the Last Judgment, to answer for the sins of the population of their cities. In becoming bishops, they had shouldered the late Roman equivalent of the 'White Man's Burden'; and they set about ruling their flocks with the sombre energy of colonial governors in a 'backward' territory. They insisted that the Christian emperors should help them: from the reign of Theodosius I onwards, pagans and heretics were increasingly deprived of civic rights and forced to conform to the Catholic Church. The sense of an otherworldly mission affected the Roman state. The Christian emperor, too, would have to answer to Christ for the souls of his subjects. In the West, this idea made weaker rulers ever more susceptible to the demands of the Catholic clergy; while, in the more firmly based eastern empire, it added yet another deep note to the swelling register of the imperial autocracy.

Wealth might be used to cover the costs of an acquittal at the Last Day. Conspicuous consumption was an inseparable part of ancient life: wealth existed to be used up in public. In the second century, the tide of surplus income had poured into public buildings; in the fourth, into the glorification of the emperor and the magnates; from the fifth century onwards, this rich flood welled into the Christian

Church 'for the remission of sins'. The rise of the economic position of the Christian Church was sudden and dramatic: it mushroomed like a modern insurance company. By the sixth century, the income of the bishop of Ravenna was twelve thousand gold pieces; the bishop of a small town drew a salary as great as that of a senatorial provincial governor.

The amazing artistic achievements of the Christian Church in the fifth and sixth centuries sprang from this redirection of wealth. The vast basilicas, covered with mosaic, hung with silk-embroidered tapestries, and lit by thousands of oil-lamps in massive silver candelabra, recaptured in their shimmering depths that sense of solemn extravagance that had once been expressed in the exuberant façades of the age of the Antonines.

Like a structure at high pressure, we can see the stresses and strains of the Roman empire of around 400 most clearly as we watch the differing impact of the ascetic movement on its provinces.

In the first place, the ascetic movement began and reached its peak in areas that had only recently come to participate in the civilization of the Greco-Roman world. The monasteries of Pachomius came to Upper Egypt only a century after a Greek-style urban life had first reached the province. In Egypt and Syria, monasticism was the bridgehead by which the fringes of the classical world entered the culture and politics of the Roman empire (see pp. 98 ff.). Provinces that the popular imagination considered as 'most Christian countries' now ringed the narrow core that a traditional pagan had thought of as civilized: in around 400, a Christian lady from Spain, whose ancestors would have been happy to go no further than Athens and Smyrna, found herself travelling to visit holy places as far east as Edessa.

Furthermore, the monastic movement affected the eastern and the western halves of the empire very differently. The parting of the ways between two types of society was further underlined, in the late fourth and early fifth centuries, by the different fortunes of monasticism. In the West, the new ascetic piety tended to 'splinter' an already divided society. It was captured by a highly articulate, but narrow, section of the aristocracy. St Martin (c. 335–97) for instance, a retired soldier of truly Syrian eccentricity, was adopted as the hero of the Gallo-Roman aristocrats, Sulpicius Severus (c. 363–c. 420–25) his biographer, and Paulinus of Nola (353–431). Later, the cult of St

Martin, and of similar holy men, lent a supernatural sanction to the dominance of the great landowner-bishops over the society of the Gallic towns.

With bishops like Ambrose and Augustine, the monastery became a means of sharpening the self-consciousness of the Catholic Church. The monastic establishment provided the bishop with the first truly professional clergy. Previously, the average Latin clergyman had been a local figure of small importance, open to pressures from his environment – a member of the local families of town councillors, or a representative of the trading community. The men who grew up in a bishop's monastery, by contrast, were cut off from their fellows by vows of chastity and poverty, and by distinctive dress; and, being often educated only on the Holy Scriptures, they no longer shared in a classical education. They had become a professional élite, with their own solidarities, their own jargon, and an acute sense of superiority over 'the world'. Furthermore, many of the spokesmen of monastic piety – men like Sulpicius Severus and the brilliant Jerome – tended to look down on the average man. They betray, in their denunciations of the 'world', of the corruption of the clergy and of the life of great cities, a Latin aristocrat's enduring contempt for the *petite bourgeoisie*, and an ancient longing for the seclusion of a great estate.

In the East, by contrast, monasticism did not stand aloof. It flowed directly into the life of the great cities. Throughout the eastern provinces the bishops had allied themselves with the monks in order to strengthen their own position in the towns. As we have just seen, the monks, with their new popularity, were the midwives of the process by which Christianity – in the late third century a minority-group dangerously limited to the towns – became the religion of the masses of the eastern empire. The growth of the monks had underpinned the narrow structure of the Christian Church. The monasteries harnessed the chronic underemployment of the towns and villages to service in the Christian Church: by 418, the patriarch of Alexandria could count on over six hundred zealous monastic retainers. The labour of the monks in hospitals, in food-supply centres, in burial associations brought the presence of the Church home to the average townsman. In Upper Egypt, the monks who had terrorized the pagans also organized an ambulance service, carrying and nursing the wounded during a barbarian invasion.

78 The new basilica. Sixth-century mosaic from
Sant'Apollinare Nuovo, Ravenna.

79 Church founding. Ecclesius, bishop of Ravenna,
presents San Vitale to Christ. Sixth-century mosaic from
the church of San Vitale, Ravenna.

Through monasticism, Christian opinion had widened its franchise in the eastern provinces. It had welcomed Coptic and Syriac
speakers as heroes of the faith; and, with the help of translations, the
bishops of the Greek towns had encouraged non-Greeks to take a
lively interest in their theological preoccupations. The city remained
the theatre where public opinion was dramatically mobilized. No-
where is this more true than at the new heart of the eastern empire –
in Constantinople. By 400 no western city could equal Constantinople as a sounding-board. Violent waves of xenophobia and religious
intolerance (usually combined) gave it a sense of identity which
Rome, still a semi-pagan city, lacked. Barbarian generals, for instance,
never rose to power in the fifth-century eastern empire, because, as
foreigners and Arian heretics, they had to skate on the thin ice of the
united Christian population of Constantinople, who showed a
'Cockney' pride in asserting their orthodoxy against such eminent
outsiders.

The difference in quality between the two parts of the Roman world
was soon put to the test. In 378, the Visigoths, who had been forced

80 A warrior society. The leader of the Alamanni appeared like this German chieftain on horseback in the fourth century; 'perched on his foaming steed, he towered over his fellows, wielding a lance of formidable proportions'. Eighth-century relief.

81 Restraint. A praying figure from a fifth-century sarcophagus in Tarragona, Spain.

across the Danube a few years previously by the onslaught of the Huns, destroyed the eastern divisions of the Roman army and killed the emperor Valens himself, at the fatal battle of Adrianople. In 406, the tribes of Germany crossed the Rhine and scattered through Gaul like a shrapnel burst. In 410, the Visigothic king, Alaric, sacked Rome. It is fashionable to regard these barbarian invasions as inevitable. Contemporaries, however, did not enjoy the detachment and the hindsight of the modern historian. The challenge from the northern world came as a surprise to Late Antique men. Up to around 400, men's attention had remained turned inwards round the Mediterranean. Civilized men had turned their backs on the north. Christianity, for instance, had expanded inside the Roman world by loosening the boundary between the 'inner barbarians' of the empire and classical civilization: the Christian bishops had not dreamt of sending missionaries to the 'outer barbarians' across the Roman frontier. Christianity had made men feel, if anything, more identified with an urban way of life: its greatest centres lay along the shores of the Mediterranean and its ethics were totally civilian. In the elegant, self-controlled classical figures of late fourth-century Christian art, there was no room for the ferocity of a warrior-society, such as existed just across the frontier. Christianity was 'The Peaceful Law'. Christian officials and Christian bishops were equally shocked by barbarians: 'What place would God have in a savage world?' wrote one; 'How could the Christian virtues survive among barbarians?' wrote another. The history of the Late Antique world after 400 is, in part, the history of how the differing societies of East and West, whose structure and attitudes had evolved in the manner described in this part of the book, would adjust themselves to the appearance of new strangers.

PART TWO: DIVERGENT LEGACIES

82 Unchanging paganism. In the countryside, paganism survived long into the sixth century; for the great landowners, whose wealth and pleasures came from the land, it was part of life. Detail of hunting mosaic from Piazza Armerina, Sicily.

IX THE WESTERN REVIVAL, 350–450

From the age of Marcus Aurelius to the middle of the fourth century, it seemed as if the centre of gravity of ancient civilization had come to rest on the eastern shores of the Mediterranean. The Latin provinces were only touched by distant ripples of the intellectual and religious storms that had raged in the eastern world. The ideas we have described in the preceding chapters were all of them first thought in Greek. When the emperor Constantius II came from Constantinople to Rome, in 357, he came as a conqueror, annexing a backward area. He entered the city with the new pomp of a Constantinopolitan *roi soleil*; and he firmly brought the 'simple-minded' clergy of the Latin world up to date by imposing his own, subtle Creed upon them. The Greek world regarded itself always as the giver. The Antiochene, Ammianus Marcellinus, came to Rome in about 385 to tell ill-informed Latin audiences about Julian the Apostate, the greatest and most Greek of recent emperors; it appeared that in the fourth century the mantle of Tacitus could fall only on the shoulders of a Greek such as Ammianus.

For a traveller from the East, to land in Italy was to enter another world, a world both grandiose and rarefied. 'There is at Rome', wrote one, 'a Senate of wealthy men. . . . Every one of them is fit to hold high office. But they prefer not to. They stand aloof, preferring to enjoy their property at leisure.' *Otium* (leisured scholarship), and the great country-villas and palaces in which this leisure took place – these were the hallmarks of the senatorial aristocracy of Rome and the Latin provinces. In Italy, great landowners had long tended to gravitate towards a private life, dedicated ostensibly to scholarly seclusion, but in fact to the protection of one's locality and the advancement of one's friends. In the fourth century, there were many families, living on their estates in Etruria and Sicily, for whom the 'crisis' of the third century had meant little, and the conversion of Constantine nothing. The correspondence of one such senator, Symmachus (*c.* 330–*c.* 402), shows an aristocrat studiously maintaining the long summer afternoon of Roman life. These letters stress the protocol of meetings of the Senate, the *punctilio* of pagan public ceremonies, the slow pomp of journeys through the provinces, the 'pot-latch' of the praetor's games that marked the début of Symmachus' son at Rome. But the majority of these letters are letters of recommendation; they were carried to court by aspirants to office, litigants, suitors, all of whom counted on the tentacular connections of an old-world Italian such as Symmachus.

This style of life was re-created by the newer nobilities of Gaul and Spain; it was fed by zealous *parvenus* from the small towns of Africa and Aquitaine. In the western society of the late fourth century, the senatorial aristocracy had come to dominate the landscape, like a skyscraper rising above hovels.

In the Latin world, also, the Catholic Church, had taken on the sharp contours of a closed aristocracy. For a longer time than in the East, Latin Christians had been a harassed minority. Like many minorities, they had reacted to this situation by treating themselves as a superior élite. The Catholic Church, therefore, had always considered itself a group 'separated' from the world. The monastic movement merely strengthened this feeling among Latin Christians; and, with the conversion to Christianity of members of the senatorial aristocracy in the late fourth century, the sense of forming a group apart, superior to the rest of mankind, reached its peak. The troubles of the Latin Church did not come from metaphysical problems as they had among the Greek bishops, but from a tendency to create splinter-groups that had broken off from the rank and file as little coteries of the elect: the Donatist Church in Africa, Priscillianism in Spain, the followers of Pelagius in Rome.

Belonging to a group vigorously committed to asserting its identity against the outside world is a spur to creativity. The senatorial aristocracy needed to maintain the high standards of culture that were supposed to mark it off from other classes; the Catholic Church, in touch with exciting movements of Greek thought and Greek asceticism, was anxious to catch up, and so was in constant need of good literature. As a result, the last generation of the fourth century and the first decade of the fifth are the third great age of Latin litera-

83 Romans of Rome. The Lampadius family, father and sons, preside over the circus races they have provided. At vast expense, generation after generation of senators dominated Rome by such means. Ivory diptych, *c*. 425.

ture. Within that short period, Ausonius of Bordeaux (*c.* 310–*c.* 395) wrote poems that show a new, romantic sense of nature, catching the vineyards on the banks of the Moselle dancing in the depths of the river. Jerome (*c.* 342–419) etched satirical vignettes of Christian Roman society – portraits of bejewelled matrons as outrageous as an Aubrey Beardsley, wicked descriptions of the clergy, written in a style that blended the denunciations of Isaiah with the low comedy of Terence, in a manner so idiosyncratic as to be the delight of pagan and Christian alike. Later, in his retreat in Bethlehem, he flooded the Latin world with the erudition he had gained from the Greeks, and with the astonishing venture of a translation of the Bible direct from the Hebrew.

Ausonius and Paulinus of Nola evolved a new style of poetry
hymn-writing. Augustine caught in his own, self-taught Latin i
the distant light of Greek philosophy: he had first read Plotin
Milan in 385, when he was still a layman in touch with the co
politan life of the imperial court. In 397, his *Confessions*, a un
history of the heart, showed the Latin language caught alight in a
whose sensibility could combine, with equal mastery, Vergil, Plo
and the rhythms of the Psalms. With the studied diffidence (
senators ostensibly writing only to amuse their friends, Sulp
Severus 'let slip' a *Life of Saint Martin*, which became a model (
future Latin hagiography. When, therefore, at the very end o
fourth century, Claudian, an Alexandrian Greek, was drawn to
to find his fortune, he was to find, in Rome and in Milan, circles w
it was possible to learn faultless Latin, and patrons who could im
on the young Greek their own very distinctive Latin enthusiasr
themselves and for the city of Rome. At the same time, Augu
was writing a great book, *On the Trinity*, that proved that it
possible for a Latin to achieve a philosophical originality unriv
by any contemporary Greek. The Latin West had come into its (

Two generations later, the western empire had disappeared
grandsons of the aristocrats who had made the renaissance of th
fourth century were subjected to barbarian kings; the West was
by an eastern observer to be 'in chaos'. The failure of the we
emperors to defend themselves against the pressure of barb
attacks after 400 and, when attacked, to win back lost territories
be largely explained in terms of the basic economic and social w
nesses of western society (see pp. 43–44). To contemporaries, f
ever, the failure of the western emperors in the fifth century
the least predictable crisis that the Roman state had ever faced
the emperors were not economic historians: they were soldiers
them, it was axiomatic that the northern provinces of the
world, northern Gaul and the Danube, were unsurpassed reser
of manpower. Throughout the fourth century, Latin soldiers
dominated the barbarian world, from Trier to Tomi. To the L
speaking soldiers from among whom the emperors were recruite
was the East, with its swollen cities and unwarlike peasantry, that
seemed the weaker part of the empire.

The reasons for the collapse of the imperial government in
West are far from simple. Questions of morale came into pla

84 Valentinian I. This fourth-century bronze statue at Barletta (much restored) may be of the last emperor who systematically patrolled and fortified the western frontiers. He was feared by the civilians for his strictness and his promotion of military personnel.

well as economic and social factors. Perhaps the most basic reason for the failure of the imperial government, in the years between 380 and 410, was that the two main groups in the Latin world – the senatorial aristocracy and the Catholic Church – dissociated themselves from the fate of the Roman army that defended them. Both groups unwittingly sapped the strength of the army and of the imperial administration; and, having hamstrung their protectors, they found, somewhat to their surprise, that they could do without them. This is an unexpected legacy of the revival we have just described. The disappearance of the western empire, therefore, was the price for the survival of the Senate and the Catholic Church.

Up to 375, the Roman army and the court life connected with the great military residences at Trier, Milan and Sirmium, had held the sectional society of the West together like an iron clamp. At that time, it was still possible for a soldier like Ammianus Marcellinus to pass along the great military roads that linked Trier to the Euphrates, speaking the easy Latin of the camps, passing without comment through all the barriers that had come to bulk large in the imaginations of the civilian population of the Mediterranean: officers of Roman and German birth, Latins and Greeks, pagans and Christians, Ammianus the soldier met them all and accepted them all. From 364 to 375, a stern Pannonian, Valentinian I, ruled the West firmly from its northern frontiers. His professional administrators were hated and feared by the Senate and, though a Christian, he studiously frustrated the growing intolerance of the Catholic bishops. He was the last great emperor to rule in the West. The events that followed his death crippled the professional *esprit de corps* of the imperial bureaucracy. The administration came to be colonized by the senatorial aristocracy with extraordinary speed and tenacity. The emperor Theodosius I (379–95), a weaker man and a landowner like themselves, opened the court to both the aristocrats and the Catholic bishops: under his non-entity of a son, Honorius (395–423), and, later, under Valentinian III (425–55), the highest offices became a virtual appanage of the Italian and Gallic nobility. The senators of the fifth century cannot be accused of having failed to participate in the political life of the empire. Far from it: they simply annexed the governmental machine to their own style of life, which had regarded politics with studied hesitation, and administration as an opportunity to look after one's friends. Amateurism, the victory of vested interests, narrow horizons – these are the ugly hallmarks of the aristocratic government of the western empire in the early fifth century.

But it was, at least, their own Roman empire. No group of Romans ever idealized Rome as enthusiastically as did the senatorial poets and speechmakers of the later fourth and early fifth centuries. The myth of Rome that was to haunt medieval and Renaissance men – *Roma aeterna*, Rome conceived of as the natural climax of civilization, destined to continue for ever – was not created by the men of the classical Roman empire: it was a direct legacy of the heady patriotism of the late fourth-century Latin world.

Yet it is characteristic of western society that this wave of

85 Paganism remembered. The classics remained part of the education of all upper-class Romans, pagan and Christian alike; but the pagan illuminator of Vergil has dwelt lovingly on just those scenes in which the pious Aeneas performed the correct pagan sacrifices, a generation after these had been prohibited by the Christian emperors. Miniature of Dido sacrificing from the Vatican Vergil (*Vat. Lat.* 3225), late fourth century.

patriotism divided men's loyalties, rather than uniting them. The most vocal patriots of the late fourth century were resolute pagans. Symmachus, for instance, treasured Rome as a Holy City. There the pagan rites that had ensured the success of the empire had survived up to 382 (when the emperor Gratian 'disestablished' the Vestal Virgins and removed the pagan altar from the Senate house). Later, Symmachus appealed frequently to the Christian emperors to continue the tacit Concordat by which Rome was tolerated as a privileged oasis of paganism – as a pagan Vatican. The Catholic bishops met these claims with bitter opposition: from Ambrose's letters answering the appeal of Symmachus in 384, to Augustine's gigantic *City of God*, begun in 413, the 'myth of Rome' stood trial in Christian circles. In this trial, Rome received only a conditional discharge. The majority of lay Christians were content to stand Symmachus on his head.

121

Rome, they replied, was of course a Holy City, and the Roman empire enjoyed special divine protection: but this was because the bodies of the Apostles, Peter and Paul, rested on the Vatican Hill. The ideology of the late fourth-century popes, and the cult of St Peter in western Europe, owe much to conscious rivalry with pagan exponents of the myth of Rome. Symmachus, paradoxically, was an unwitting architect of the medieval papacy.

But even the most enthusiastic Christian patriot had to admit that the cult of the Rome of St Peter was, in part, an attempt to lay a ghost. The last pagans of Rome reminded Christians, at the very last moment, of the unregenerate, pagan past of the empire. They charged the myth of *Roma aeterna* with sinister associations. Throughout the Middle Ages, just beneath the surface of the Holy City of St Peter, there always lurked, as an indelible stain on the Christian imagination, the idea that Rome had been 'the Devil's City'. In Constantinople, the Roman empire was accepted without question as a Christian empire. All that the bishops of the medieval West could do, by contrast, was to conjure up the pale clerical shade of a 'holy' Roman empire.

The society of the western provinces of the Roman empire was fragmented. In the late fourth century, boundaries had hardened, and a heightened sense of identity had led to harsher intolerance of the outsider. Senators who had participated in an impressive revival of high standards of Latin literature were little inclined to tolerate a 'barbarian'. Bishops who could boast Ambrose, Jerome and Augustine as colleagues were in no mood, either, to tolerate those outside their Catholic Church. As a result, the barbarian tribes entered a society that was not strong enough to hold them at bay, but not flexible enough to 'lead their conquerors captive' by absorbing them into Roman life.

This is the significance of the so-called 'barbarian invasions' of the early fifth century. These invasions were not perpetual, destructive raids; still less were they organized campaigns of conquest. Rather, they were a 'gold rush' of immigrants from the underdeveloped countries of the north into the rich lands of the Mediterranean.

The barbarians were vulnerable. Their numbers and military capacity might win the battles: but they were in no position to win the peace. The Visigoths crossed the frontier at the Danube in 376 and turned their attention to Italy in 402, under their king Alaric.

86 The soldier saint. In the Middle Ages, St Martin was portrayed quite frankly as a knight. His late Roman biographer, however, a typical civilian, tried to gloss over the fact that Martin had ever been a soldier. Twelfth-century detail of the frontal of Montgonry.

87 The 'integrated' barbarian. A Vandal chief, Stilicho, was commander-in-chief and self-appointed regent to the western emperor Honorius from 395 to 408. Contemporary opinion was violently divided about his policy towards the Visigoth Alaric: had he used money and alliances to protect the empire, or to 'enrich and aggrandize the savages'? Wing of ivory diptych, c. 400.

The Vandals entered Gaul and Spain in 406–09. The Burgundians settled down in the Middle Rhône Valley after 430. These successes were impressive and totally unexpected. Yet the conquering tribes were divided against each other and within themselves. Each had produced a warrior-aristocracy, far removed from the tastes and ambitions of their own rank and file. These warrior-aristocracies were quite prepared to leave their 'underdeveloped' fellow tribesmen behind, and to become absorbed into the prestige and luxury of Roman society. Theodoric, king of the Ostrogoths (493–526), was later in the habit of saying: 'An able Goth wants to be like a Roman; only a poor Roman would want to be like a Goth.'

In those areas of the Balkans controlled by the court of Constantinople, the lessons which the Roman military experts had learnt in the fourth century were applied successfully. A judicious combination of force, adaptability and hard cash neutralized the effects of the Visigothic immigration. The Visigothic warrior-aristocracy was 'integrated' by being offered posts in the High Command, or set to tasks that served the purposes of east Roman diplomacy. When Alaric was deflected from the Balkans to the West, however, he faced a society with neither strength nor skill. The senators had failed to pay their taxes or to provide recruits for the Roman army; yet, when they were asked, in 408, to pay for a diplomacy based on subsidies to Alaric, that might have covered their military weakness, the Senate rejected the proposal as smacking of 'appeasement' of the despised barbarian: 'This is a slave's contract, not a subsidy.' Noble words: but two years later these patriots would have to pay three times as much as they had been asked to contribute, in order to ransom their own city from the Visigothic king. A strident chauvinism and a refusal to negotiate with the barbarians led to the Sack of Rome by Alaric in 410. It was not an auspicious beginning to the coming century of Roman-barbarian relations.

So much for the Roman senators. As for the Catholic Church, its bishops were the spokesmen of the prejudices of the average Mediterranean townsman. Townsmen dreaded the barbarians: but they also knew and disliked soldiers. Their Christianity was not so much pacifist, as resolutely civilian. Sulpicius Severus went to great lengths to disguise the fact that his hero, St Martin of Tours, had ever been a Roman officer: only in the far more military society of the Middle Ages did artists gladly portray him as a knight. There was no room for the soldier-saint in the fourth-century Latin congregations, and, one may suspect, they cherished little enthusiasm for the Roman army.

As for the barbarian, he was the successor of the Roman soldier: he was branded as a man of war, tainted with 'ferocity of soul', in the midst of the peace-loving 'Sheep of the Lord'. He was also a heretic, for the Danubian tribes had adopted the strong Arian Christianity of that region.

The barbarian settlers in the West found themselves both powerful and unabsorbable. They were encapsulated by a wall of dumb hatred. They could not have been 'detribalized' even if they had wanted to be, because as 'barbarians' and heretics they were marked men. The intolerance that greeted the barbarian immigration, therefore, led directly to the formation of the barbarian kingdoms. To be tacitly disliked by 98 per cent of one's fellow men is no mean stimulus to preserving one's identity as a ruling class. The Vandals in Africa from 428 to 533, the Ostrogoths in Italy from 496 to 554, the Visigoths in Toulouse from 418 and later in Spain, up to their conversion to Catholicism in 589, ruled effectively as heretical kingdoms precisely because they were well hated. They had to remain a tight-knit warrior caste, held at arm's length by their subjects. Not surprisingly, the word for 'executioner' is the only direct legacy of two and a half centuries of Visigothic rule to the language of Spain.

The Franks were the exception that proved the rule. They were latecomers: Frankish war-bands rose to prominence only in the late fifth century, long after the establishment of the other Germanic tribes. They did not come as conquerors: they had infiltrated in small numbers, as mercenaries. Above all, they kept clear of the highly articulate populations round the Mediterranean. Northern Gaul remained the centre of gravity of the Frankish state. Southern bishops and senators found it easier to accept such comparatively insignificant strangers. As a result, the Franks felt free to become Catholics. At the Merovingian court of the sixth century, Roman and Frank butchered and married each other without discrimination; and Gallo-Roman bishops, well aware of the continued existence of strong Arian states to their south (the Visigoths in Spain held Narbonne, and the Ostrogoths of Italy expanded into Provence), hailed the unsavoury warlord of the Franks, Clovis (481–511), as 'a new Constantine'. The very success of the distant Franks, indeed, is an indication of how little tolerance the Roman population of the Mediterranean were prepared to extend to the barbarian states on their own doorstep.

This state of affairs is usually treated as inevitable by historians of western Europe in the fifth and sixth centuries. But it is not the only way in which a great empire can treat its barbarian conquerors. Northern China, for instance, was more thoroughly occupied by the barbarians of Mongolia than ever the western provinces of the Roman empire were by the Germanic tribes. Yet in China the barbarians 'went native' within a few generations, and continued the Chinese imperial tradition without a break, from dynasty to dynasty. The Visigothic, the Ostrogothic and the Vandal kingdoms of western Europe were never absorbed in this way: they survived as foreign bodies, perched insecurely on top of populations who ignored them and set about the more congenial business of looking after themselves.

The barbarian invasions did not destroy west Roman society, but they drastically altered the scale of life in the western provinces. The imperial government, now settled in Ravenna, lost so much land and taxes that it remained bankrupt up to the time of its extinction in 476. The senators lost the income of their scattered estates. They were able to make good some of their losses by rack-renting and chicanery in the areas where their power was strongest. The great landowners of Italy and Gaul, whose power rested so heavily on the peasantry, were a threatened rump of the affluent absentee-landlords of the previous century. Communications suffered. In the late fourth century, senatorial ladies from northern Spain travelled freely all over the eastern empire; in the fifth century, a bishop writing in Asturia hardly knew what happened outside his own province. In western Europe, the fifth century was a time of narrowing horizons, of the strengthening of local roots, and the consolidating of old loyalties.

Immediately after the Sack of Rome the Catholic Church asserted its unity: schism was forcibly suppressed in Africa after 411; in 417 the Pelagian heresy was chased out of Rome. Men felt they could no longer afford the vigorous religious strife of a more secure age. The last pagans, therefore, rallied to the Church. Their culture and patriotism now contributed to hardening the boundaries of Catholicism: in the mosaics placed in S. Maria Maggiore in 431, for instance, the Temple in the background of the scene of Christ's Presentation at the Temple is the old *Templum Urbis*. Leo I (440–61), the first pope to come from the old-fashioned countryside of Rome, praised Rome as the see of St Peter in language that echoes exactly the punctilious devotion of Symmachus to the Capitoline gods. In a world increasingly conscious of the presence of the non-Roman, Catholicism had become the single 'Roman' religion.

With this new religious solidarity went a strengthening of local ties. This can be seen most clearly in Gaul. The provincial aristocracy of Gaul had always been both loyal to its homeland and successful as suitors at court. The tradition begun at Trier in the fourth century merely continued with gusto in the more outlandish barbarian courts of the fifth. Sidonius Apollinaris (*c.* 431–89) included among his skills the gentle art of gaining a petition by tactfully losing at backgammon whenever he played against the Visigothic king Theodoric at Toulouse.

88 Eternal Rome. The circus is unchanged (*cf.* Ill. 83), but *Roma* has become a majestic allegorical figure, placing her hand on the shoulders of the consul. Wing of the sixth-century ivory diptych of the consul Basilius.

89 The new barbarian ruler. Though of barbarian workmanship, this plaque shows King Agilulf of the Lombards in a manner that follows exactly the ceremonial of a late Roman triumph: winged Victories carry banners (*cf.* the Archangel in Ill. 111), other barbarians bring tribute (*cf.* Ill. 100), the king is greeted as a deliverer by the inhabitants of his cities – indicated by the slender towers at the sides (*cf.* Ill. 15). From the helmet of King Agilulf, probably Turin, beginning of seventh century.

The newly established barbarian kingdoms provided ample scope for the gifts of the courtier. Despite their prejudices, the local senators quickly realized that to have a strong man with an effective military force on one's doorstep has its advantages. The Romans exploited the divisive effects of new wealth among the barbarian nobility. They tended to back the kings against their unruly followers by encouraging them to establish strong dynasties on the imperial model. A typical example of the survival of the scholar-bureaucrat at a barbarian court is Cassiodorus (*c.* 490–*c.* 583), who was a minister of Theodoric the Ostrogoth and his successors in Italy. Cassiodorus framed the royal edicts in traditional style; he skilfully presented Theodoric and his family as 'philosopher kings' (for he could hardly have called them legitimate Roman rulers); and he even wrote a *History of the Goths* that presented the tribe in general, and the family of Theodoric in particular, as co-operative participants in the history of the Mediterranean, from the time of Alexander the Great onwards.

More bluntly, the Romans came to recognize that the devil you know is better than the devil you do not. In Aquitaine, the Visigothic presence sheltered the villas of Sidonius and his friends from tribes

such as the Saxons who were known to have terrorized Britain. In 451, it was the local senators who persuaded the Visigoths to join the Roman army in halting the avalanche of Attila's Huns. It was the presence of the barbarian garrisons in Gaul which ensured that, while in Britain not a single Roman estate-name survived the Saxon invasion, the villages of the Garonne and the Auvergne bear to this day the names of the families that owned them in the fifth century.

The politics of Roman courtiers at the new barbarian courts were local politics. The idea of a united western empire was increasingly ignored by men who genuinely loved the smaller world of their province. In the letters of Sidonius Apollinaris, we see the rooted passions of the gentleman-farmer emerging behind the mask of the senator's *otium*. In the letters of Symmachus, we see only a style of life: in those of Sidonius, we move through a distinct landscape – his beloved Clermont: 'Where pastures crown the hill-tops and vineyards clothe the slopes, where villas rise on the lowlands and castles on the rocks, forests here and clearings there, headlands washed by rivers . . .'

Sidonius became bishop of Clermont in 471. For, to lead one's local community in the conditions of the late fifth century, one had to become its bishop: only the solidarity of the Catholic community linked the local nobleman with his dependants; and the prestige of new-built basilicas and shrines of martyrs maintained the morale of the little towns of southern Gaul.

Paradoxically, the spread of the monastic movement eased the delicate transition from senator to bishop. The monastic communities at Lérins, Marseilles and elsewhere were filled by noble refugees from the war-torn Rhineland. These communities provided the clergy of southern Gaul with men of high class and culture. A touching belief that the holy man interceded for the average sinner had enabled Sidonius to live at ease with his failings while he was a Catholic layman, and the idea of the monastic vocation, far from involving him in a total denial of the world, had merely instilled in Sidonius and his circle the sober sense that for all things there was a time and a season, and that with old age a man had to shoulder spiritual responsibilities. Having sowed their wild oats, having founded their families, Sidonius and his friends passed into the austere gerontocracy of the Catholic Church. They took with them frank memories of good dinners, of martyrs' vigils that had ended, in the cool of the morning, with a *fête champêtre*, of spacious private libraries stocked with the classics, where the Fathers of the Church were tucked away discreetly at the women's end.

Yet as bishops, landowners like Sidonius completed the silent revolution that made the countryside of Gaul Christian and Latin-speaking. Their slow work of evangelizing the peasantry finally tipped the balance from Celtic into Low Latin as the spoken language. Hence a double movement, visible all over the West. Classical culture became more narrow and esoteric. The towns of Gaul hardly provided enough schooling: a century after Ausonius and his colleagues had turned out thousands of classically educated young men from the thriving university city of Bordeaux, the study of Latin literature had shrunk into the private libraries of the few great senatorial villas. From being the property of any well-to-do man, a classical education became the badge of a narrow oligarchy. As this restricted aristocracy of letters entered the Church, in the late fifth and sixth centuries, classical rhetoric attained an unparalleled flamboyance. When the bishops met on solemn occasions or wrote to each other, the 'grand style' rose in them: their smooth flood of phrases, 'polished as onyx', would have been as impenetrable to the contemporary outsider as they are now to the modern reader. The letters and *jeux d'esprit* of bishops such as Avitus of Vienne (*c.* 490–518) and Ennodius of Pavia (513–21), and the rhetoric of the edicts framed by Cassiodorus are typical products of this movement: shorn of their privileges, their wealth curtailed by confiscations, ruled by outsiders, the senators of the West showed, in a rococo zest for Latin rhetoric, their determination to survive and to be seen to survive.

Yet, as bishops, these men had to maintain the morale of their less-educated flocks. To do this, they would adopt a 'humble' style. In Gaul, for instance, the sixth century is an age of lives of saints written in simple Latin. Usually we remember bishop Gregory of Tours (538–94) as the author of a *History of the Franks*, notorious for its vivid accounts of the unsavoury manœuvres at the Merovingian court of Franks and Romans alike. But we come closer to Gregory in his lives of the great protector-saints of Gaul. Here we have figures dear to his heart: an awesome heavenly nobility, like himself, inflexible in retribution but, also like himself, minutely preoccupied with details of the life of the average man in town and country.

With this strengthening of local ties affecting all provinces, Italy became the 'geographical expression' that it was to remain. North and south were already sharply divided. The bishops and landowners of the north were long used to the presence of a military, barbarian government. They found themselves at home at the court of Odoacer (476–93) and, later, of Theodoric at Ravenna. But to cross the Apennines was to enter a different world, where the court was far away, and the past all-pervading. In Rome, vast Catholic basilicas and long memories eclipsed the present. A double oligarchy of senators and clergymen – now closely interrelated – maintained the splendid isolation of the city. Characteristically, the Senate resumed its powers of minting coins, which it had lost since the end of the third century. As soon as the western emperors were removed, in 476, the emperor's image was discreetly replaced by a picture of Romulus and Remus suckled by the wolf, and the motto *Roma invicta*, 'Unconquered Rome'. In this way, the romantic ideology of *Roma aeterna* filled the vacuum of sovereignty created by the end of legitimate Roman rule in Italy. We see the 'Romans of Rome' of the late fifth and early sixth centuries on their consular ivories: tense figures, dwarfed by the vast shade of Rome.

In his great family library, the senator Boethius (c. 480–524) was able to draw on intellectual riches that had first been garnered in the Latin renaissance of the fourth century. He laid the foundations of medieval logic with the help of the books owned by his great-grand-fathers; and, in his *Consolation of Philosophy*, he still puzzles us by the tranquillity with which a staunchly Christian Roman aristocrat of the sixth century could reach back for comfort, in the face of death, to the pre-Christian wisdom of the ancients. Theodoric executed Boethius for alleged treason in 524: in so doing he struck shrewdly at the most eminent, and so at the most isolated, member of an unreconciled group. The proud and lonely Boethius went to his death for having lived so very well a life that had preserved everything in Rome – everything except an emperor.

After 533, a Roman emperor returned to the western Mediter-ranean. Justinian's armies conquered Africa, at a blow, in 533: by 540, his general, Belisarius, entered Ravenna. Justinian's campaigns were hamstrung by the revival of the Persian menace (in 540), by the terrible plague that raged intermittently (from 542 onwards), and by the collapse of the Danubian frontier with the first Slav inva-sions of 548. Nevertheless, east Roman rule continued in Ravenna, Rome, Sicily and Africa for centuries to come.

The unexpected intervention of the imperial armies proved the acid test for the relative strength of the discrete groupings of Roman society in Italy and Africa. For the senatorial aristocracy, Justinian's reconquest was a disaster. An eastern autocrat with efficient tax-collectors was not the emperor they had bargained for. For this brittle oligarchy, Justinian's wars in Italy marked the end of a way of life. The bitter recriminations of the Italian senators were welcomed by the cowed nobility of Constantinople: they come to overshadow the pages of Procopius of Caesarea's classic description of the Gothic Wars, and they erupted against Justinian in the impotent fury of the same author's *Secret History*.

Yet we should not judge the success of Justinian in the West merely by the fate of this one highly articulate group. The Catholic clergy did not share the resentments of the Roman Senate. The Roman Church was delivered from Arian rule, and absorbed the vast pro-perties of the Arian churches. Under Gregory I (589–603) Rome was its pope. In this complex man, the clerical streak in the Roman aristocracy, anticipated in the priests and popes in his own family,

90 A clerical dynasty. Typical of sixth-century western society: Euphrasius, the bishop, built the church, the archdeacon Claudius provided the Gospels, and his son, the candles. Mosaic in the basilica at Istria.

came to the top. From the vast private library of his relative, pope Agapetus (535–36), Gregory gained a familiarity with Augustine, for instance, such as was possible only for an aristocrat. The flame of Platonic mysticism, which had passed from Plotinus to Augustine, flared up again in the sermons of Gregory. Mindful of the past habits of his class, Gregory kept open house to the Roman people: he lavished the carefully guarded revenues of the Church on corn for the poor, and on living allowances for distressed senators. His epitaph called him 'God's consul'. Yet Gregory was not merely a survival from the aristocratic past of Rome. He lived in an age when Rome had been integrated for over a generation into the east Roman empire. Gregory's austerity, his sensitivity to popular devotion (shown in the miracle-stories in his *Dialogues*), his austere sense of the bishop's office (shown in his *Pastoral Care*), make him a Latin version of the forbidding holy men who, as patriarchs of Constantinople, Antioch, Jerusalem and Alexandria, held the great cities of the East for the Byzantine emperors.

Seen from Rome, however, the position and aims of the Roman emperors of the East were interpreted in a characteristically Latin atmosphere. The only portraits of Justinian and Theodora that we possess – the court-scenes on the mosaics of S. Vitale at Ravenna – are grouped round the altar of a Catholic church; for to the Catholic bishops of Italy, the empire existed for their own benefit. These bishops were the direct heirs of the Roman Senate. The *libertas*, the privileged position, of the Roman Senate had formed one of the ideals of the Roman aristocracy in the early sixth century: imperceptibly, the ideal was taken over by the Roman clergy. It made itself felt throughout the Middle Ages. This is the most far-reaching and paradoxical outcome of Justinian's reconquest.

For Justinian entered the western Mediterranean, with grandiloquent opportunism, to regain what he considered to be the lost provinces of *his* empire: he had little sympathy for the *libertas* of the Roman Senate, and he was quite prepared to browbeat any pope who did not co-operate with his ecclesiastical schemes. Yet the Byzantine armies stayed on for centuries in Italy, to protect the privileges of the Roman Church. In western eyes, the east Roman empire existed to provide military protection for the papacy. The wary easterners who arrived at Ravenna as exarchs (viceroys of the emperor) were greeted, in Rome, as upholders of the *Sanctissima*

Respublica – the Most Holy Commonwealth. The eastern empire, therefore, came to be invested with the halo of a 'holy' Roman empire: not Augustus, but Justinian, the pious Catholic of the mosaics at S. Vitale, was the model of the renewed Roman empire of Charlemagne. Justinian was the direct, if unwitting, ancestor of the idea that a 'Christian commonwealth', a Holy Roman Empire, should always exist in western Europe to serve the interests of the papacy and to secure the *libertas* of the Catholic Church.

A city, its habits and associations, changes slowly. In seventh-century Rome, the members of the clerical oligarchy of the city still proceeded to their churches as the consuls had processed in the early sixth century – greeted by candles, scattering largesse to the populace, wearing the silken slippers of a senator. The Lateran Palace was so called, it was thought, because 'good Latin' was still spoken there. In their great basilicas, the popes continued to pray for the *Romana libertas*. The idea that western society had to recognize the predominance of a sharply defined, clerical élite, as the emperors had once recognized the special status of members of the Roman Senate, was the basic assumption behind the rhetoric and ceremonial of the medieval papacy: like the last warm glow of evening, the late Roman senator's love of *Roma aeterna* had come to rest on the solemn façade of papal Rome.

91 The ruling city. The walls of Constantinople built by Theodosius II. By AD 800 these walls had already withstood several sieges.

XI 'THE RULING CITY': THE EASTERN EMPIRE FROM
THEODOSIUS II TO ANASTASIUS, 408–518

When Rome was sacked in 410, three days of public mourning were declared at Constantinople. The eastern emperor, Theodosius II, did little else to help the western capital: but his ministers soon took good care to surround Constantinople with great walls. Throughout the Middle Ages, the Theodosian Wall, which still towers above the outskirts of modern Istanbul, summed up the impregnable position of Constantinople as the surviving capital of the Roman empire. It was not breached by an enemy until 1453.

Under Theodosius II, Constantinople became 'The Ruling City'. The emperors came to reside permanently in the Great Palace by the Bosphorus. The ceremonies of the court became part of the rhythm of the daily life of the city. The great issues of policy – peace and war, heresy and orthodoxy, parsimony or affluence – hammered out by the emperor and his advisers in the great 'Hall of Silence' (the *silention*) would spill over into the bazaars of the city: when the emperor appeared in his box in the Hippodrome, the supporters of the rival racing-stables – the Circus-factions of 'Greens' and 'Blues' – would applaud or criticize his decisions in rhythmic shouting. The inhabitants of Constantinople, cocksure and contentious, were frequently reminded that politics was no game. Constantinople lay on the Balkan side of the Straits of Marmara, only 270 miles away from the storm-centres of the Danube estuary. Nearly every generation, the inhabitants of the city would watch, from their great wall, the trail of smoking villages left by barbarian war-bands. In the fifth and sixth centuries, Constantinople combined the pride of a city-state and the high morale of an outpost with the resources of a vast, Near Eastern empire.

Yet at the beginning of this period, Constantinople was still very much an alien northern capital. As we have seen (on p. 112), the deepest division in the society of the fourth century was between north and south, not between east and west: civilians of the Mediterranean were all of them equally distant from the military court that paced up and down the northern highroads. Theodosius II himself came from a family of Latin generals; and in 438 he instigated the great Latin compilation of imperial laws known as the 'Theodosian Code'.

As long as the court maintained its connection with the military, Latin was its spoken language. Even to a Greek, Latin had always been the language that expressed the majesty of the state – like 'law French' in late medieval England, Latin was the imposing jargon of the administration. This Latin was learnt by the east Romans in schools, though it had no connection with the living language – we have papyri showing Egyptian boys doing passable translations of Vergil, as we ourselves do in a modern school. The foundation of Constantinople had brought the majesty of the Roman state into the heart of the Greek world: but the Greeks who learnt Latin in increasing numbers in the fourth and fifth centuries did not do so to visit the old Rome in the West, but to enhance the grandeur of Constantinople, their 'New Rome'.

Like the Egyptian obelisks in the Hippodrome and the Greek classical statues in public places, Latin survived quite naturally in Constantinople as part of the grandiloquent façade of a world empire. The Latins themselves, however, slowly disappeared in the course of the fifth century. In Constantinople, the whole tendency, from the third century onwards, for the Roman empire to become a military autocracy was silently reversed. At the end of the fifth century, the Roman army had been eclipsed as a political force by a cabal of high administrators, palace officials and retired bureaucrats resident in Constantinople. The two greatest emperors of the age, Anastasius (491–518) and Justinian (527–65), were both civilians of the new type: Anastasius had been a palace official until late middle age; and Justinian, though the nephew of a Latin soldier from the Balkans, had become thoroughly 'civilized'. The heights of statecraft and culture reached under these two remarkable men sum up the slowly matured achievement of the civilian governing class. In the course of the fifth century, the Roman empire had found its way to a new identity, as the empire of Constantinople.

The scholar-gentry of the Greek towns had been the architects of this silent revolution. They filled the minor offices of the great financial and legal ministries. One such, John of Lydia, made one thousand gold pieces in his first year, under Anastasius – 'and that was honestly come by', he added! He learnt Latin; he wrote poems in praise of his chief of staff; he retired to write an antiquarian mono-graph, *On the Magistracies of the Roman State*. The tenacious conserva-tism of a classically educated gentleman which, in the western pro-vinces, had been focused in vain on a mirage of *Roma aeterna*, invested the efficient framework of the eastern empire with a necessary patina of long traditions and quiet pride. In Constantinople, scholarship and letters were an adjunct, not an alternative, to statecraft. Agita-tion against an unpopular tax, for instance, made decisive use of a play on the subject 'in the manner of Euripides'. Even the Platonic tradition which, in the West had passed on only its otherworldly and mystical aspects, retained in Constantinople its concern with government. Policies were hotly debated: in 399, a future bishop, Synesius of Cyrene, could outline a policy of excluding the barbarians in his speech *On Kingship*; in his *Secret History* of about 550, Procopius of Caesarea could draw up, for a politically alert faction, a notorious 'Black Book' of the reign of Justinian. These men continued from their master Thucydides a tradition of writing contemporary history. Their varied careers gave them ample opportunity for this: Priscus of Panium left a keenly observed description of his mission to the court of Attila in Hungary; Procopius (died 562), as secretary to Justinian's victorious general Belisarius, a deeply felt *History of the Wars* of his time.

The civilian governing class of the east Roman empire learnt the arts of survival in a hard school. The rise of the great nomad empire of Attila (434–53), whose power stretched from the plains of Hungary to Holland and the Caucasus, marked a turning-point in Roman history. This was the first emergence, in the northern world, of a barbarian empire on a par with the Romans. The fourth-century Roman empire had still thought of itself as embracing the known civilized world. The Sassanian empire was the only other organized state it knew. Like a policeman, it patrolled the small-time criminals on the utmost fringes of civilization. In the fifth century, this myth of the 'middle kingdom' was shaken. The east Romans came to learn that their empire was one state among many, in a world that had to be scanned anxiously and manipulated by adroit diplomacy. In the mid-fifth century, Olympiodorus of Thebes (in Egypt) is the first colourful representative of a long tradition of Byzantine diplomats:

he went on missions as far apart as Rome, Nubia and the Dnieper – accompanied by a parrot who spoke pure Attic Greek.

The emperors insisted that diplomacy, being as important as warfare, should cost as much. At exactly the same time as the western senators were allowed by their ruler to burn their tax-arrears, the senators of Constantinople were being made to sell their wives' jewellery to pay for the subsidies that eventually brought down the empire of Attila. For the bureaucracy was often headed by ruthless outsiders, who depended on imperial favour alone. Marinus the Syrian, the praetorian prefect of Anastasius, was typical of the financial experts who saved the eastern empire when its western half had collapsed: 'And at night also, he had a pen-and-ink stand hanging beside his bedside, and a lamp burning by his pillow, so that he could write down his thoughts on a roll; and in the daytime he would tell them to the emperor and advise him as to how he should act.' (Zachariah of Mitylene, *History*.)

The emperor's palace officials – above all the great eunuch-chamberlains – were recruited from far beyond the traditional governing class. Thus the backstairs government of the palace did not cut off the emperor from his subjects. Far from it: it was part of the secret of Byzantine rule that this all-important, shadowy fringe was often more closely in touch with the feelings of the provincials than was the polished mandarinate of the bureaucracy.

Constantinople had become the goal of ambitious provincials placed far beyond the Greek core of the empire from which the traditional bureaucracy was recruited. At the end of the fifth century, Daniel, a young Syrian from Mesopotamia on his way to practise asceticism in Jerusalem, was warned in a vision to go instead to Constantinople: with its great churches and collection of relics, the 'Ruling City' had become a 'Holy City'. Less spiritual young men would make the same decision: Daniel had hardly set himself up on a pillar – in imitation of the Syrian practices of Simeon the Stylite – when he was chatting away in Syriac with a fellow oriental who had become the emperor's head-waiter! The history of Constantinople in the late fifth century was shaped by such gifted immigrants. The emperors could not do without the new ferment of prosperity and

92 The imperial majesty. The empress Ariadne, wife of the emperor Anastasius (491–518). Ivory diptych, c. 500.

93 The east Roman bureaucrat. A statue set up (during the fifth century) in his home town in Asia Minor.

94 A father of the faith: icon of *apa* Abraham. The monastic leaders were the focuses of intense local loyalties and the true arbiters of the theological controversies of the sixth and seventh centuries, for they were treated as the spiritual directors of the laity, and as the guardians of the traditions of the faith. Sixth- to seventh-century panel painting from Bawit, Egypt.

THE MOTHER OF GOD   95 Pagan: Isis suckling Horus. Third-century Coptic frieze.

96 Christian: Mary suckling Jesus. Fifth- to sixth-century tombstone from Fayum, Egypt.

97 The Syrian achievement. The pilgrimage centre at the monastery established around the pillar of St Simeon Stylites. The architecture continues the flamboyant style of the late second century (*cf*. Ill. 3), but the emperor is showing his loyalty, not to his home town, but to the local saint. Main portal of the south façade of Qalat Sem'an, *c*. 480.

talent along the fringes of the classical world. It was not enough that the empire of Constantinople should be a Greek empire: it had also to embark on the delicate quest for an identity as an eastern empire in the true sense. The cultural and theological storms that bulk so large in the ecclesiastical history of the late fifth and sixth centuries were part of the attempt of the cosmopolitan society of the eastern empire to find its balance.

'The one maxim of extended empire, a wise and salutary neglect' (Burke), just could not be applied to the provincials of the fifth-century empire. Egypt, for instance, had entered the mainstream of cultural life. Its richer peasants and small-town notables were typical provincials of a new east Roman society. They had created from scratch an exuberant and idiosyncratic sub-classical art – Coptic art. The most typical creation of the Egyptian Christians of these centuries was the icon: an abstracted, simplified image on which the worshipper could concentrate, looking straight into the charged eyes of his spiritual Father – Menas, Anthony or some other hero of Egyptian Christianity. The Egyptian patriarchs, Theophilus and Cyril, led the Greek world. The Council of Ephesus in 431, in declaring that Mary was the *Theotokos* – 'She Who gave birth to God' – ratified the fervour of the Copts, who had worshipped her as such, suckling the new-born Jesus. This prototype of the most tender scene in medieval art was a Coptic adaptation of Isis suckling the infant Horus.

143

The heyday of the Syriac-speaking provincials came a little later. Under Anastasius, Syrian merchants were trading as far apart as Gaul and central Asia. The financial wizard of the court, Marinus, was a Syrian. Syrian masons developed a filigree delicacy in carving stone surfaces. Above all, it was the Syrians who had filled the Greek world with music. Romanos the Melodist came to Constantinople from Edessa: he poured an imagery and a dramatic sense, that reach back directly to the most ancient Semitic East, into the chants of the Byzantine Church. In the Hagia Sophia, bands of Syrian monks would disturb the Sunday congregation by striking up, in long-drawn melodies, the litanies of their distinctive adoration of the crucified Christ. Syrian farmers had colonized the hillsides of the Anti-Lebanon with olive trees. The emperor established a huge pilgrimage centre on the spot where Simeon had squatted on his pillar. The vast complex of Qalat Sem'an, greater than Baalbek and as exuberant, was a gesture of recognition from the 'Ruling City' to the provincials, on whose industry the economy of the east Roman state depended.

Compared with these ancient Christian centres, Constantinople, only recently weaned from a military, Latin past, was a colourless newcomer. But to be a 'Ruling City' it had to lead the empire in doctrine also. The emperors hastily forced it to the fore. At the Council of Chalcedon in 451, the emperor Marcian took advantage of a trend in Greek opinion and of the support of Leo, the bishop of Rome, to humble the patriarch of Alexandria, and so to secure the position of Constantinople as the leading Christian city of the empire. The settlement arrived at in Chalcedon did violence to some of the deepest currents in Greek Christian thought of the time. The equilibrium of eastern Christianity was brutally upset. For the next two centuries, the emperors faced the uphill task of restoring the balance, sometimes by palliating, sometimes by by-passing 'the accursed council', without going back for a moment on the initiative which their 'Ruling City' had won at Chalcedon.

The issues raised at the time of Chalcedon were not trivial, for the council had seemed to split the human from the divine element in the person of Christ. The emperor's part in the council was partly political; but resistance to its doctrine was heartfelt and not a 'cover' for social grievances, much less for strivings for national autonomy by the eastern provinces. Centuries of Christian experience in the provinces had been flouted by the upstart capital. For the pious Greek, Copt and Syrian,

Christ was the prototype of the redeemed man. To what extent, these men would ask, did God deign to take up and transform human nature, to lift it out of its frailties, in the person of Christ? If human nature was totally transformed and made one with God's nature in Christ – hence the convenient theological label 'monophysite' (*monos*, single; *physis*, nature) – then the average man could eventually hope to be saved in the same way: he, also, would be transformed. The average man looked round him. He saw the holy man: if frail human nature could be endowed with such supernatural power in this life, then surely the divine nature in Christ had been that much more absolute and indivisible? Who but a totally divine Being could stand between mankind and its towering enemy, the devil? To emphasize, as the doctrinal statement of pope Leo – his *Tome* – had done, the humbled, human element in Christ, shocked the Greek reader. For this attitude threatened to leave God's work of salvation half-done: to condemn human nature itself to the position of an untransformable residue, a bitter dreg at the bottom of the unbounded sea of God's power.

It has been said that the Council of Chalcedon divided the empire irreparably; that it rendered inevitable the loss of the eastern provinces to Islam in the seventh century. This view is so lofty that it misses the quality of the life of the sixth-century eastern empire entirely. The exact opposite was the case. Despite the explosive nature of the issues involved, despite the fact that the ecclesiastical traditions of whole provinces were mobilized on both sides, the empire remained united. We can learn a lot about the resources of the east Roman state by seeing how this could be so.

In the first place, the imperial administration had created a unified state: men paid their taxes and prayed for the success of the emperor whatever their shade of theological opinion. It was possible for a merchant from Alexandria to cash a cheque in a bank at Constantinople – a service which no medieval state could offer until thirteenth-century China. The culture of the empire had few deep barriers. Men felt free to move from the provinces to the capital without losing touch with their roots. Scratch a Greek poet like Cyrus of Panopolis, and we find an Egyptian devoted to the martyr-saint of his home-town; and even Procopius, the Byzantine Thucydides, spoke Syriac and believed that the prayers of Syrian holy men played their part in holding the eastern frontier of the empire. Throughout this

98 Secular: a wild-beast hunt in the circus of Constantinople. Detail from the ivory diptych of Areobindus, 506.

99 Religious: relics carried in procession. The patriarch on his high carriage holds the box with the relics, as he passes the imperial palace (note top left, the icon of Christ over the main gate). They are preceded, left to right, by the senate, the emperor and the empress. Spectators in the top window of the palace swing sweet-smelling incense. Fifth-century ivory plaque.

period, we are dealing with a society which had experienced strong and intimate pressures making for centralization, for standardization, for economic and political solidarity. The concern for the 'peace of the Church', that haunted the emperors of the late fifth and sixth centuries, should not be seen as a desperate attempt to heal a divided empire: rather, the emperors hoped to make the partisan bishops and their flocks live up to standards of unity and obedience that were patently being realized in every other field but religion.

The prestige of the emperor was even increased by religious uncertainties, for all attempts to achieve unity passed through the court. The emperor gained a position that he was to hold throughout Byzantine and early Russian history: he was the keystone of the great vault of the 'peace of the Church'. It was a position gained by sheer hard work. When conspirators wanted to assassinate the emperor Justinian, they knew how they would find him: every night he would be sitting in an alcove of the Great Palace, discussing with holy men and bishops the intricacies of his subjects' beliefs.

The reign of the emperor Anastasius (491–518) sums up the quality of the east Roman empire at this time. Anastasius was a pious layman, who used to give lectures on theology. He was the only late Roman emperor ever to abolish a tax – the gold tax on the cities. By rigorous professionalism, he died with a surplus of thirty-two thousand pounds of gold. We catch a glimpse of him in the local chronicle of Edessa: in this faraway frontier town, the emperor was

147

very much 'the little father' of his people. Even to his theological opponents, he was 'Anastasius, the good emperor, the lover of monks and the protector of the poor and afflicted.' In his religious policy, he was unmistakably a product of east Roman society. Though a sincere 'monophysite', he worked, above all, for religious peace. He banned extremists of every kind.

In 517, Anastasius received a delegation of priests from Rome that showed how far apart the western and the eastern halves of Christendom had already drifted. The Catholic Church in the West had become a closed élite – like a colonizing power in underdeveloped territories, it regarded itself as obliged to impose its views, by force if need be, on the unregenerate 'world'. Reinforced by their aristocratic background, its senator-bishops towered above an increasingly passive and uncultivated laity. They were in the habit of telling lay-rulers what to do. The Roman legates told Anastasius that he should impose the Catholic faith on his provincials with the firmness of a crusader. To the east Roman emperor, such advice came from another, more barbarous world. Anastasius wrote back: he would not make the streets of his cities run blood so as to impose the views of one faction on all the rest. His business was not to outlaw half his empire; it was to find a formula by which the rich spectrum of the beliefs of his subjects could be blended: 'Peace I leave with you,' he quoted to the pope, 'my peace I give you.'

Here we have a parting of the ways: western Europe in the Middle Ages was dominated by the idea of the Church Militant; Byzantium, a stable and united empire beneath its apparent disagreements, long skilled in the politics of *consensus*, stuck to the grand ideal of the 'peace of the Church'. In his last sentence, Anastasius was to address the pope in words that are an overture to the majesty of Justinian: 'You may thwart me, Reverend Sir; you may insult me: but you may not command me. . . .'

EMPIRE AND BARBARIANS

100 Ideal. Relief from the obelisk of
Theodosius I in the Hippodrome in
Constantinople, *c.* 390.

101 Reality: a coin of the emperor,
maybe given as largesse, worked into
a piece of barbarian ornament. Gold
pendant set with a coin of
Valentinian II, seventh century,
found in Staffordshire.

Anastasius, as we have seen, passed naturally into the imperial office after a lifetime of service in the palace. Justinian, by contrast, was a *nouveau riche* of east Roman culture. With his uncle Justin, he had drifted into the 'Ruling City' from a Balkan village: his native language was Latin. When Justin, as captain of the guard, became emperor by accident, Justinian, as heir apparent, threw himself into the life of Constantinople. It was in Constantinople, one suspects, and not in his village, that Justinian first learnt to value Latin as the imperial language. In Constantinople he gained a deep acquaintance with Greek theological literature and opted for the anti-monophysite party. In Constantinople, also, he dabbled in the *demi-monde*: he played politics with the Circus-factions and he took his wife, Theodora, from a family connected with the racing-stables. As a young man, he was anxious to conform to the backward-looking ethos of the resident aristocracy: he wooed the senators of Constantinople, and on becoming consul, he humbly dedicated his ivory diptychs to them, in Latin – 'Small gifts these, in price, but heavy with respect.' His first act on becoming emperor was to form a commission to reorganize the Roman law. When Justinian succeeded his uneducated uncle in 527, it seemed as if the 'Ruling City' had absorbed yet another zealous *parvenu*.

The great Nika Riot of January 532 – so called from the slogan *Nika* (Conquer!) adopted by the mob – changed the tempo of his reign dramatically. It was the worst explosion of violence in east Roman history. Angered by Justinian's ministers, people and Senate united against the emperor. Half the city was burnt. As the flames rose round the Great Palace, only Theodora was able to rally her panic-stricken husband – 'The purple is a glorious winding-sheet,' she said.

Theodora's exclamation became the keynote of Justinian's reign. Somewhat like a 'liberal' tsar of nineteenth-century Russia who had been the object of an assassination plot, Justinian turned his back on the traditionalist elements in Constantinople. No east Roman emperor exploited with such zest the resources of the autocracy.

The stage-set of traditional ceremonies inherited from the Roman past was wheeled away to leave the emperor alone in his majesty: the consulship, which the young prince had valued so highly, was abolished in 541. The life of the court was expanded, its ceremonial

102 Justinian and his ministers. Mosaic in San Vitale, Ravenna.

103 Theodora. Mosaic in San Vitale.

MAXIMIANVS

made more awesome; Theodora travelled with four thousand attendants – twice as many, that is, as were used by the Ottoman sultans in the nineteenth century. Justinian appealed to the Christian provincials of his empire, away from the neutral façade of the educated aristocracy. He posed as the 'most Christian emperor'. His fanaticism was all-embracing and, usually, prudently directed against isolated minorities, such as the surviving pagans. After 533 public opinion was mobilized in a crusade against the heretical Arian kingdoms in the West. Public morality was upheld by meticulous legislation against blasphemy and gambling. Theodora looked after her own by founding a hostel for reformed prostitutes. Throughout the empire, Justinian placed churches whose style, based on the basilicas of the capital, was uniform from Ceuta, on the Atlantic coast of Morocco, to the Euphrates. In an age of primitive communications, Justinian ensured that by memorable gestures of Christian piety and Christian intolerance, and above all through money, stone- and mosaic-work, the presence of the autocrat was brought home to the man in the street.

These gestures were crowned by the rebuilding of the Hagia Sophia, burnt down in the Nika Riot. Justinian could have restored the old church, as had been done before; but he was in no mood for so limited a project. Instead, he called on Anthemius of Tralles and Isidore of Miletus to build a revolutionary new church. These men were typical members of the technological élite of the Greek world: as a mathematician, Anthemius went beyond Euclid in exploring the parabola; and Isidore had studied the great monuments of Rome. The Hagia Sophia combined the two traditions: in the Roman imperial grandeur of this church, a Greek tradition of abstract thought was frozen into stone, with the hovering domes. When he entered the new church, however, Justinian struck the more popular note of the Byzantine man in the street: 'Solomon!' he cried, 'I have outdone thee!'

The 530s were an exceptionally favourable interlude for the east Roman state. Justinian exploited the opportunities in the international situation to the full. The imperial fleet that sailed from the Bosphorus to Africa in 533 was presented as a crusade to deliver the lost provinces of the Roman empire from their heretical overlords. The prodigious windfall of the quick collapse of the Vandal kingdom in Africa proved Justinian right: the Vandal king was paraded in

104 'The salvation and glory of the Romans': medallion celebrating the reconquest of Justinian. The emperor is shown on horseback, as in the great days of the imperial recovery of the third century (cf. Ill. 15). Medallion of Justinian, 534–38 (copy).

triumph in the Hippodrome. When he issued the second edition of his Digest of Roman law in 534, Justinian revived in his proclamation the grandiloquent epithets of a Roman conqueror: 'Justinian . . . conqueror of the Vandals, of the Goths, etc.' The commission that produced this great work included the same ministers – Tribonian and John of Cappadocia, the praetorian prefect – for whose heads the mob had chanted in the Nika Riot of only two years previously. Justinian and his friends were more firmly in the saddle than ever before. In 539, the Ostrogoths had been driven out of Rome, and were suing for peace; and in Constantinople, Justinian appeared on a mosaic, surrounded by his faithful advisers, 'with gay and festive expression'.

Few emperors established their threatened position with such inspired opportunism. But in so doing, Justinian had cast his own shadow over the rest of his reign. Compared with the grandiloquent euphoria of the 530s, the remaining twenty-five years of his reign seem a sinister anti-climax. For modern scholars, Justinian has been trapped in his own image. His astute manipulation of the resources of propaganda has been taken at face value. Hence he has gained the reputation of being a romantic idealist, haunted by the mirage of a renewal of the Roman empire; and the difficulties of the succeeding years have usually been presented as the nemesis of a grandiose policy.

153

Justinian is a less sinister, if more complex figure. He sought glory while the going was good, because he sorely needed it to maintain his position; and he had the genius to realize the vast resources available to an east Roman emperor of the early sixth century – an almost numinous past history, a full treasury, an unrivalled supply of human talent in every field. But the history of his reign was written – as was so often the case in the Roman empire – by the alienated and the embittered. Justinian had betrayed the traditionalist governing class of the empire; he had outflanked them in a policy of flamboyant glory; but it was they who remained to chronicle, with bitter attention, every detail of the shipwreck of the young emperor's hopes.

The 540s were a catastrophic decade. In 540, Khusro I Anoshirwan, the shah of Persia, broke his truce with Byzantium. The eastern garrisons had been neglected for the western wars. The shah fell on Antioch, the second city of the empire, and, having cynically offered to sell it to Justinian, plundered it and marched slowly home again, emptying the cities of northern Syria with impunity.

In his reaction to the revival of the menace of Persia, Justinian showed that he was no dreamer. The war in Italy was instantly relegated to a backwater. In coming years, Justinian was prepared to spend more money on impressing one Persian ambassador in Constantinople than on all the armies in the reconquered western provinces. From the Black Sea to Damascus, the emperor's foresight was crystallized in stone. Justinian's fortifications along his eastern frontier are the most refined example of Roman military architecture. They still stand in the desert as tangible reminders of the overriding priority of the Near East in the policies of the east Roman state.

While the eastern provincials were sheltered from the consequences of Justinian's western commitments, his fellow countrymen in the Balkans felt the strain directly. The Balkan garrisons were stripped to provide levies for the western armies. The Danube frontier became permeable again. In the 540s the Slavs raided deep into Roman territory. From 559 onwards Constantinople itself was frequently menaced by the revival of great confederacies of Turkic nomads – heirs to the empire of Attila: first the Bulgars, followed by the Avars. To regain the remote Latinity of Italy and Africa, Justinian weakened the living Latin core of the east Roman state in the Balkans. The Slav settlement of the Balkans was a direct consequence of Justinian's western ambitions. While his portrait survives in Ravenna, Justiniana Prima, the capital of the reorganized Balkans which he had founded under his own name (somewhere, perhaps, in southern Serbia), vanished so completely, after the invasions of the late sixth century, that nobody knows for certain where it stood.

The natural catastrophe of the Great Plague formed the background to these reverses. The epidemic began with a vicious outburst between 541 and 543, and remained endemic throughout the Mediterranean up to the 570s. It was the worst attack until the Black Death of 1348. It knocked the bottom out of the grandeur of the 530s.

From 540 onwards, Justinian sank himself into a dogged routine of survival. The true measure of the man and of the east Roman state was not the *belle époque* of 533 to 540: it was the quality revealed in the harsh years that followed. The Justinian of the Byzantine tradition is not the young adventurer of the 530s, whose portrait we all know from the mosaics in his reconquered capital of Ravenna: it is the slightly uncanny old man, who worked until dawn every night in the seclusion of the Great Palace – the 'many-eyed' emperor, 'the sleepless one'.

Throughout the wars and the plague, Justinian's financial officers kept the money coming in – not by increasing the taxes, but by ensuring that the rich paid up promptly. Money was now turned to a technology of survival. Fortifications replaced men along the frontiers. Diplomacy was stretched to its utmost to cover a lack of military power. Only under Justinian did Christian missionaries begin to be used as agents of Byzantine 'cultural imperialism' in the northern world: baptism and the arrival of clerical advisers now became the routine consequences of an alliance with the emperor.

Warfare, also, became more specialized. Later in the sixth century, Byzantine generals wrote manuals which show how closely they had observed and copied the new cavalry tactics of the nomads. War, for such men, was like hunting – a delicate art in which bloodshed was no substitute for skill. The perpetual emergencies from 540 onwards created, among the generals and diplomats, an experimental frame of mind that culminated, in the mid-seventh century, in the development of 'Greek fire' in the Byzantine navy – the most devastating application of technology to warfare in the early medieval period.

Inside the empire, Justinian continued to tinker ceaselessly. He experimented with new forms of revenue: after 541, the manufacture of silk, for instance, became a government monopoly. He ruthlessly cut away dead wood. An immensely costly system of free government transport, inherited directly from the time of Augustus, was axed. Only one road was now maintained – significantly, the great highway leading across Asia Minor to the eastern frontier. By the end of Justinian's reign, the exuberant, involuted façade of the late Roman state, whose generous and many-sided reserves Justinian had tapped with gusto before 540, had been stripped down to its steel framework.

Because of this drastic overhaul, Justinian's reign did not end in failure. Far from it: in 552 the Ostrogothic resistance was shattered in a single, skilfully planned and executed engagement; in 554, large areas of southern Spain came under Byzantine rule; after 560, Africa was pacified, and Byzantine fortresses held a frontier more ambitious than that held by the emperor Trajan. The Danube line was protected by a cat's-cradle of alliances. The truculent Khusro I had been checkmated. Within the empire, the villages of Palestine and Syria were as prosperous as ever. International trade provided opportunities for revenue: the fleets of the patriarchs of Alexandria sailed to Cornwall in the early seventh century; and the beautiful gold coins of Justinian and his successors found their way as far afield as Sweden, Peking and Zanzibar.

The most fateful legacy of Justinian to succeeding generations was precisely the extent of his success. He had proved that autocracy worked as a short-term remedy for the ills of the Byzantine state. Rather like Philip II, toiling endlessly in the Escorial, this 'sleepless' figure fostered the illusion that one man could solve the problems of an empire.

Personal government sapped the quality of the imperial bureaucracy. The scholar-administrators of the early sixth century had tended to be hidebound and resistant to high taxation. But they had guaranteed a degree of continuity and had fostered the participation in government of the educated governing classes of the Greek world. Justinian's gifted professionals ended by whittling down the links between a bureaucracy made up increasingly of imperial favourites, and east Roman upper-class society at large. These men got in the taxes; but the steady press of talented young gentlemen to Constantinople came to a halt – imperial service was too abrasive a profession.

As a result of increased professionalization throughout the sixth century, the old structure of provincial life disappeared. The immemorial right of the Greek town councils to levy the taxes on their locality vanished. By the end of the sixth century, town councillors in their solemn robes were no more than a childhood memory. Deprived of their old focus of allegiance, the towns of the eastern empire fell into the hands of their bishops and their great landowners. The populace turned to theology and to gangsterism. Savage clashes between Circus-factions in all the towns of the empire shocked and puzzled contemporaries in the late sixth century, much as they still puzzle historians.

Justinian had cut away too much of the old tissues of east Roman society. Only his choice of efficient servants and his boundless curiosity saved him from isolation. And in his old age, Justinian's grip was relaxed with disastrous results. His successors had nothing to fall back on but his tradition of palace-government: Maurice (582–602) and Heraclius (610–41) were spectacular emperors; but they had to govern their empire through a *camarilla* of hated and disunited courtiers and through their relatives.

The weakness of the east Roman empire, however, was that it was an essentially civilian state. Its strength lay in its tax-payers. Throughout the sixth century, agriculture had been maintained at a high level; and new opportunities for commerce had been opened up. Until the reign of Heraclius, the emperors had sufficient funds to allot to substitutes for military strength, fortification and diplomacy. But money could not create soldiers. Maurice and Heraclius both revived the older, militaristic tendencies of the Roman empire. They took the field in person. But they found they had not enough men to lead. Hence the strange combination of fragility and grandeur in the Byzantine empire after Justinian: a sprawling territory of rich countrysides and prosperous cities found itself caught between the hammer and the anvil of two professedly military empires – the warrior-hegemony of the Avars to the north and the fearsome nobility of Persia to the east. How could the traditions of civilian autocracy, inherited and heightened by Justinian, resist consistent pressure in the Near East from Persia, whose art, a Roman observer once remarked, 'shows nothing but scenes of hunting, of bloodshed and of war'?

The challenge of Persia dominated the late sixth and early seventh centuries in Byzantium. In the course of the sixth century the Roman empire had become a Near Eastern state. Rome was an outpost: 'If God does not move the heart of the emperor to send us a general or a governor,' wrote the pope in the late sixth century, 'then we are lost.' Even on the distant shores of the western Mediterranean, Byzantine rule meant incorporation in an oriental empire. The Byzantine outposts in the West were like mirrors, casting the light of the eastern Mediterranean far into the darkness of early medieval northern Europe. Isolated and grandiloquent, the kingdom of Visigothic Spain nevertheless moved to the rhythms of Byzantine life: its rulers eyed the eastern empire closely as a model and as a potential menace. In northern Europe, every great church was hung with Byzantine silks; liturgical books were written on Byzantine papyrus; relics were cased in Byzantine silverwork; legends and liturgy were of eastern origin; saints were, inappropriately, buried in shrouds of Persian silk, showing the griffins of Zoroastrian mythology and the hunting feats of pagan shahs in the Iranian plateau.

The centre of gravity of the Christian world still lay in the eastern Mediterranean. One of the earliest archbishops of Canterbury, Theodore (669–90), was a Byzantine subject from Tarsus (southern Turkey). On the Northumbrian coast, the Venerable Bede (c. 672–735) drew his Biblical erudition from the works of African bishops who had written to persuade Justinian in faraway Constantinople. When Gregory I wished to cement an alliance with the Lombards, he sent their queen a flask of oil from the shrine of the Holy Cross at Jerusalem. On the Atlantic coast of Spain, an unknown lady was buried with a similar flask. For the barbarians of Europe, Jerusalem was still the centre of the world: and Jerusalem was a Byzantine city.

Fragile though these Byzantine outposts were, they ensured that the southern shores of the Mediterranean belonged to an empire whose heart lay in the Near East. This is the long-term significance of Justinian's reconquests in the West. From Gibraltar to Gaza, the inhabitants shared with the eastern provinces a common loyalty to the Roman emperors, a common piety, a common idiom in ornament, a common stable coinage. They were already sharply distinguished from the underdeveloped territories to their north – northern Spain, Gaul and northern Italy. The diagonal division of the Mediterranean into two societies, so that a Near Eastern empire came to stretch like the long, sloping plane of a wedge from Antioch to the valley of the Guadalquivir, was the most marked feature of the western

105 Affluence: a banquet scene from a sixth-century manuscript, the *Vienna Genesis* (*Cod. theol. graec.* 31).

Middle Ages. The division was begun by the conquest of Justinian. Except at Rome and Ravenna, the Muslims stepped straight into the inheritance of the Byzantine exarchs. Even the fateful entry of the Moors of Al-Tarik into Spain in 711 – the notorious 'betrayal of Don Julian' – was a last, fatal stroke of diplomacy by an isolated Byzantine governor, Julianos of Ceuta: his ill-judged use of the Muslims as barbarian mercenaries was in the best traditions of Byzantine foreign policy laid down by Justinian.

In the Near East, Justinian did not stand by himself. His achievements were rivalled by the revival of Persia under Khusro I Anoshirwan – 'Khusro of the immortal soul'. A contemporary, the historian Zachariah of Mitylene, saw this clearly when he watched the celebrations in the Hippodrome of Constantinople in 534. The Vandal king was paraded before Justinian in an unparalleled triumph: 'But ambassadors of Khusro, king of the Persians, were there, and they sat there, and they saw these things. . . .' It is time for us, also, to look at the sixth-century world through more eastern eyes.

In the palace of Khusro I Anoshirwan at Ctesiphon (on the Euphrates, thirty-five miles south of modern Baghdad), three empty seats stood beneath the royal throne. These were for the emperor of China, for the great khagan (the ruler of the nomads of central Asia), and for the Roman emperor, in case these rulers came, as vassals, to the court of the king of kings. The three thrones summed up the vast horizons of the Sassanian empire. Persia was the link between East and West. It was from sixth-century Ctesiphon that Indian science and Indian legends – particularly the story of the Buddha (known in the West as the story of Barlaam and Josaphat – from 'Boddhisattva') – filtered into the Mediterranean. Chinese travellers knew Persia well, while their knowledge of the Roman world stopped at Antioch. In the early Middle Ages, Persian *condottieri* defended the northern frontiers of China. It was they who introduced into the Far East the skills of cavalry-warfare, learnt in constant conflict with the nomads of central Asia.

For Persia was, above all, a central Asian power. The settled, agricultural life of the Iranians, especially in the rich lands of Gurgan (classical Hyrcania) by the Caspian, had always been threatened by nomads from the steppes of Turkestan. It was still remembered, in the sixth century, that both the Persians' religious leader, Zoroaster, and their greatest king, Darius, had died fighting against central Asian raiders. Traditional Persian society had as acute a sense of the 'barbarian' as did the Romans. Khusro I never celebrated his capture of Antioch on coins: but when, in 568, he crushed the great nomad empire of the Hephthalites (the White Huns) on his northern border, a special issue proclaimed, 'Iran delivered from fear'. The Central Asian frontier was the military laboratory of the Late Antique world. It was against the nomads that the Persian aristocracy developed the 'cataphract' (the heavily armoured horseman), a predecessor of the medieval knight. Typically, this new technique was known to the Romans by the name first used in the Syriac slang of Mesopotamia – 'boiler boy': the eastern provincials of Byzantium, witnessing these iron-cased warriors from Transoxiana, passed on their Syriac name to the Roman army, in its Latin translation – *clibanarius*.

In central Asia, also, the civilization of Persia dominated early medieval Bokhara and Samarkand. The sub-Iranian society of

106 Khusro I Anoshirwan (531–79). Unlike Justinian the civilian, the shah is shown as a warrior. He sits on his throne holding his drawn sword. Detail from the so-called Cup of Khusro, sixth century.

107 The *clibanarius*, the armoured horseman. Second- to third-century graffito at Dura-Europos.

108 Mani, as shown by his devotees in the Turfan oasis. A religious leader born in southern Mesopotamia, his message spread through Syria to the Roman empire and through Central Asia to China. Eighth- to ninth-century wall painting from Khocho (Turfan), China.

Soghdia, which included these great towns, linked East and West. In the sixth century, Soghdian middlemen sold the knowledge of the silkworm to the emperor Justinian, just as, a century previously, they had sold Roman techniques of glass-making to the emperor of China. In this island of Persian culture, the two forms of Christianity that had grown up in Persian-dominated Mesopotamia – the radical asceticism of the Manichees (the followers of Mani, see below, p. 164) and the humane Christianity of the Nestorians – flourished until the Mongol invasions of the thirteenth century. In the oasis of Turfan, in the south-western Gobi Desert, Manichaean liturgies of the tenth century still presented Heaven as a court ruled by the same protocol as that devised for the palace of Khusro I Anoshirwan in distant Ctesiphon.

Westerners, reared on Herodotus, regard a confrontation between the Roman empire and Persia as natural. Yet, given the time-honoured commitment of the Iranian governing classes to central Asia, the constant westward pressure of the Persian empire against the

162

frontiers of Byzantium throughout the sixth century is exceptional. Previously the Roman empire had been saved by the sheer size of its rival. The Persian empire uncoiled, like a dragon's tail, across the 'harsh and rugged land' east of the Zagros range, as far as the Oxus, Afghanistan and the Indus valley. The austere, arid plateau of Iran – the Castile of the Near East – was the traditional heart of the Persian empire. Here a rigid Zoroastrian orthodoxy was unchallenged in the sixth century. Here, also, the great traditional families had held despotic sway. In the holy cities of Istakhr and Persepolis, and on the rock-faces of Naqsh-i-Rustam, the Sassanian king of kings drew on traditions that reached back to the Achaemenids: Shapur I placed himself next to Cyrus and Darius. In Mesopotamia, by contrast, the Iranian governing class travelled down into a foreign country. At the court of Ctesiphon, the nobility lived in a separate quarter, in palaces well stocked (so a Chinese traveller observed) with ice: they yearned for their summer retreat in the great hunting-lodges of Holwan, in the mountains of Media proper. Outside Ctesiphon, the   163 population spoke Syriac. They were mainly Nestorian Christians, living alongside important Jewish communities. Many a Persian aristocrat, in the late sixth century, 'went native' in Mesopotamia by becoming a Nestorian Christian, and so had to learn to chant his Psalm book in Syriac.

Mesopotamia, however, was the economic heart of the Persian empire. The shahs derived two-fifths of their revenues from it. Here was an ancient urban society that provided the skills on which the court depended. Since the raids of Shapur I on the Roman empire in the 250s, Persian-controlled Mesopotamia – especially Khuzistan in southern Iraq – was permeated with settlements of deportees from the eastern Mediterranean. Its towns provided the shahs with their architects and engineers. The weavers on whom the glory of sixth-century Sassanian silks depended lived in them; and so did the financiers. The term for the land-tax originated in the Aramaic of the fifth century B C, it was still in use under the Sassanians (as we can see from the Jewish Talmud), and it emerged as the official, Arabic designation – *kharaj* – for the land-tax on which the finances of the Arab empire depended.

Mesopotamia was an area of immense creativity. From the third century A D, the views of its religious leaders had impinged on the conservatives of both the Roman and the Persian empires. Mani, the founder of Manichaeism (216–77), was a typical product of this environment. Living at the crossroads of Asia, he had felt challenged, as no religious thinker round the 'little frog-pond' of the Mediterranean had felt challenged, to create a self-consciously universal religion. He was aware of the confrontation between the world religions of East and West: the Buddha and Zoroaster figure alongside Christ in his message. Manichaean missionaries reached northern Spain in the fifth century; by the seventh, they were in Peking. In the same enriching environment, Nestorian Christianity settled down as the only truly oriental church. Excluded from the orthodox Roman empire, the Nestorians struck up a delicate *modus vivendi* with the Persian governing class. Nestorian clergymen followed the Persian-dominated trade-routes as far apart as Fukien and Ceylon: the Syrian Christians of Kerala (southern India) looked to Ctesiphon. In 638, the Nestorians offered a statement of their beliefs to the emperor of China: it was a quite unmistakable echo, in a strange environment, of the arguments first propounded by Christian Apologists in Antioch and Alexandria. Throughout the early Middle Ages, the Syriac-speaking clergy of Persian Mesopotamia carried many intriguing scraps of culture between the Far East and the Mediterranean.

In Mesopotamia, moreover, a crucial development for medieval and modern Europe took place: the final crystallization of rabbinic Judaism. Protected by the shahs from Christian intolerance, the rabbis of Mesopotamia gained intellectual pre-eminence over their cowed brethren in Palestine. They compiled the Babylonian Talmud. At a time when the emperor Justinian was laying down which version of the Scriptures the Jews should be allowed to read in the synagogues of his empire, the rabbis of Ctesiphon were free to conduct a vigorous polemic against the Christian doctrines of the Trinity and the Virgin Birth. Searching criticisms aired in the cities of Persian Mesopotamia soon filtered along the caravan routes into Arabia, where they had a decisive influence on the epoch-making monotheism of Muhammad.

Mesopotamia, therefore, stood to one side in the Persian empire. Its towns, its contacts with the Mediterranean, its high proportion of settlers from the Roman empire, marked it off from the arid, land-locked and jealously traditionalist world of the Iranian plateau. The shah called himself 'King of Kings of Iran and of the non-Iranian territories'. In the first centuries, these did not overlap. Yazdkart I (399–421), for instance, was popular with his Mesopotamian subjects: he was detested by the Iranian conservatives, to whom he was known as 'Yazdkart the Sinner'. His successor, Vahram Gur (421–39), was known to the Byzantines as a truculent persecutor of the Christians: in Persia, he was treasured throughout the Middle Ages as the bluff King Hal of Persian history – the perfect Iranian gentleman, a passionate hunter, generous to the nobility, an upholder of Zoroastrian orthodoxy.

In the late fifth century, however, the traditionalist world of the Iranian plateau collapsed and Mesopotamia came into its own. After seven years of famine, the shah Firūz (459–84) was killed with his whole army in a rash campaign against the Hephthalite Huns. The 'Famine Days of Firūz', and the total defeat of Persia by the nomads of Central Asia, were remembered as the worst tragedy in Persian history before the Arab invasion. It was the end of the Iranian *ancien régime*. Undermined by defeat, threatened by an outburst of apocalyptic radicalism – by the movement of Mazdak, a religious leader, whose teachings had sparked off *jacqueries* at the time of famine – the survivors of the conservative nobility rallied round the young shah, Khusro I, for protection: they gave him his title, Anoshirwan (Immortal Soul), when, as crown prince, he massacred the followers of Mazdak in 528. Khusro protected the nobility, but on his own terms. He tied the Zoroastrian clergy and the great families to his court. A new class of professionals gradually took over the administration. Many were Christians: they came from Mesopotamia, not from Iran.

Khusro was remembered in the Near East as the just king *par excellence*. He had his own views on the purpose of this justice: 'The monarchy depends on the army, the army on money; money comes from the land-tax; the land-tax comes from agriculture. Agriculture depends on justice, justice on the integrity of officials, and integrity and reliability on the ever-watchfulness of the King.' While his contemporary, Justinian, was also remembered as 'the just', it was as a codifier of law: Khusro, by contrast, realized the formidable Near Eastern ideal of the long-armed king. 'Go write letters to them,' he told the Nestorian patriarch, on hearing of a rebellion in Khuzistan, 'that if every rebel does not have the goodness to keep quiet, I shall go up against them with sword, bow and arrow, and I shall kill every man who persists in his insubordination against me – be he a good Zoroastrian, a Jew or a Christian.'

The forty-eight years of harsh rule by Khusro I and the thirty-seven years of brittle grandeur under his grandson, the erratic Khusro II Aparwez – ('the victorious', 591–628), mark the true birth of the Middle Ages in the Near East. At least a generation before the arrival of the Arabs, Persian society had been weaned from its past, and given a form that lasted far into the Middle Ages. Just as, in the West, the emperor Augustus was remembered as an insubstantial shade beside the palpable figures of Constantine and Justinian, so, in the Near East, the shahs before Khusro are remote fairy-tale figures. The history of the medieval Near East began with Khusro – Kesra to the Arabs, Khusraw in modern Persia.

The caste-ridden, aristocratic structure of the fifth-century world was loosened. The courtier-gentleman – the *dekkan* – emerged as the backbone of Persian society. The *dekkan* stood for a new way of life. He was a substantial landowner, a soldier and a courtier. Like its Byzantine equivalent, the new administrative élite created a new culture that was a blend of preciosity and professionalism. The *dekkans* were eclectic: Khusro I patronized translations both of Greek philosophy and of the courtly fairy-tales of north India. While their predecessors in the fourth and fifth centuries had been shown, in massive rock-carvings, locked in epic combat with enemies or wild beasts, these courtiers played games: chess, polo, and, in hunting, the delicate skill of falconry replaced the big game hunt of earlier centuries. The great archetypal figures of the kings disappear. Exquisite, embroidered silks were more to the taste of the Persians of the late sixth century. Above all, in the court of Khusro Anoshirwan, we leave the age of the gods for the age of men. Zoroastrianism became merely a conservative sentiment. The shahs are no longer shown receiving their powers face to face with their god, Ahura Mazdah: Khusro appears only with his courtiers. The mystique of the sixth century was the *farr-i-padshahan* – the nimbus of the king of kings. Long after Persia ceased to be Zoroastrian, the *dekkans* maintained this reverence for their monarch.

These developments determined the course of Near Eastern history for the next five hundred years. Like a submerged rock, the court society created in Persia by Khusro I Anoshirwan and perfected by Khusro II Aparwez deflected the course of the Arab empire. 'The Persian conquest of Islam' in the eighth and ninth centuries was expressed in the foundation of the Abbasid califate at Baghdad, within sight of the deserted halls of Ctesiphon. It was the last efflorescence of forms of life created, in the Near East, in the Late Antique period.

In many ways, the reformed Persian society of the late sixth century gravitated round a sub-Byzantine court whose centre lay in Mesopotamia. Byzantine architects helped to build the palace at Ctesiphon; the Byzantine land-tax provided the model for the reforms of Khusro I; Aristotle was adopted at this time to redefine points of Zoroastrian ethics; Mesopotamian Christians, who spoke the same Syriac language as did their neighbours across the frontier, transmitted Byzantine medicine, philosophy and court manners to the Sassanian capital. Often, the frontier stood wide open. In 527, Nestorian Christian professors from the Persian city of Nisibis were welcomed in Constantinople: in 532, Platonic philosophers from Athens stayed with Khusro at Ctesiphon. Byzantium and Persia were drawn closer together by the wealth and creativity of the populations of the Fertile Crescent. The constant, exhausting state of war that

109 The Persian afterglow in Central Asia: a Hindu deity painted in the Persian manner, in Khotan. Seventh- to tenth-century panel painting from the Hu-Kuo convent in Chinese Turkestan (ancient Khotan).

reigned between them from 540 to 561, 572 to 591 and 602 to 629, was the result of two societies forced into proximity.

Khusro I unwittingly destroyed the balance of the Persian empire. He had tacitly abandoned Iran and Central Asia for Mesopotamia. Deprived of their former horizons, the Sassanian shahs of the late sixth and early seventh century were forced to bid against Byzantium – a state economically if not militarily superior to their own – for the hegemony of the Near East.

The amazing feature of the sixth century was the rapid rise of Persia on the eastern frontiers of Byzantium. From being the Sick Man of the Near East in the late fifth century, Persia caught up with its rival. At the beginning of Khusro I's reign, Persia was a parasite of Byzantium: the shah used his formidable war-machine to extort money from its richer neighbour by blackmail. The looting of the Byzantine provinces by Khusro I 'primed the pump' for Persian emergence out of bankruptcy. Under Khusro II, Persia became the financial giant of the Near East, and the shah the centre of a fairy-tale court.

Khusro II was the fateful heir of the policies of Khusro I. He had the makings of an emperor of the united Near East. Largely estranged from the nobility of Persia proper, he had been put back on the throne, in 591, with the help of Byzantine mercenaries. He was surrounded by Christians. His wife, the beautiful Shirēn, and his financial wizard, Yazden of Kerkuk, were Nestorians. He shrewdly addressed his propaganda to the Christian populations on both sides of the frontier: he ascribed his successes to the protection of St Sergius, the patron saint of the Syriac-speakers and of the Arabs of the Fertile Crescent. In this half-Christian form, the shadow of the king of kings lengthened across the western section of the Near East.

Khusro II found his chance in 603. He invaded the Byzantine empire, ostensibly to avenge the fallen emperor Maurice and to uphold legitimate rule against the usurper Phocas. The dream of the new Mesopotamian court, to reunite the Fertile Crescent as in the days of Cyrus, Xerxes and Darius, seemed near accomplishment. Antioch fell in 613, Jerusalem in 614, Egypt in 619; by 620, the Persian watch-fires were visible, across the Bosphorus, from the walls of Constantinople. And Khusro II had come to stay: Persian governors in Egypt have left tax-documents in Pehlevi which take up traditions of Persian domination that had lapsed in Egypt – for a mere nine hundred years! – since the days of the Achaemenids.

The Byzantine empire was saved by the skills developed in the reign of Justinian. Heraclius mobilized the popular feeling of Constantinople. He fought brilliant campaigns with a small, ferociously disciplined army. He vanished into the Caucasus with every bit of money that he could lay his hands on – even the treasures of the Hagia Sophia were melted down to coin gold pieces – to conduct a subsidy-diplomacy, after the model of Justinian, on the northern doorstep of Persia. In alliance with the Khazars, Heraclius struck south, in 627, into the heart of Khusro's empire. The great palace of the king of kings at Dastgerd was burnt; and Khusro, discredited by this lightning raid on the unprotected estates and holy cities of the Zoroastrian clergy and nobility, was murdered by his ministers in 628.

The war was a catastrophe for the settled populations of the Near East. The prosperity of the villages outside Antioch ended abruptly after 613; Alexandria was left partly deserted; the conquered territories were mercilessly taxed and stripped of their skilled labour. As for Persia, the gamble of Near Eastern rule had failed. There was nothing left to fall back on. Persia was unable to survive military defeat at the hands of the Arabs after 641. Its heart was burnt out. When the Muslim armies reached the Iranian plateau, they found anarchy.

But the most fatal weakness of all was that neither great empire was prepared for what followed – for the explosion from the primitive south of the Fertile Crescent associated with the rise of Islam.

The spectacular wars between Persia and Byzantium had been fought out along the northern tip of the Fertile Crescent: from the Caucasus to northern Mesopotamia, the countryside had been covered with expensive fortifications; armies had marched and counter-marched across its familiar landscape. By contrast, the soft underbelly of the Fertile Crescent had been defended by a fragile network of alliances among the neighbouring Arab tribes: east of Damascus at Djabiya, the Ghassanids – the Banu Ghassan – policed the frontier as Byzantine feudatories; at Hira, the Lakhmid kingdom formed a buffer state, shielding Ctesiphon itself from the desert that lay only a hundred miles from its walls.

In their last great war, both sides had forgotten about the Arabs. From being carefully nourished protégés of the great powers, the Arabs of the frontiers were in danger of becoming the pariahs of the Near East. The delicate defensive system, that had maintained a balance between cultivated land and the desert from southern Iraq to Sinai, had been washed away. The Roman forts stood deserted. The sheiks were no longer tempted to control their followers. Already during the Persian occupation, Beduin raided with impunity up to the gates of Jerusalem.

If the two great powers had forgotten about the Arabs, the Arabs themselves felt drawn closer than ever before in their history to the rich towns and disturbing ideas of the settled countries to their north. In Mecca a merchant oligarchy had begun, about 600, to invest large sums in direct trade with southern Syria and Hira. Meccan caravans contributed to an unexpected 'boom' in the economic life of Damascus, Bostra, Gerasa (Jerash) and Gaza. These southern towns throve when northern Syria lay desolate. Meccan merchants (the least successful among them being a certain Muhammad) were well established outside Damascus. The steady pressure of the Arab merchant-adventurers up into the undefended southern frontiers was a warning that already all roads might lead to Mecca.

110 The courtly ethos. The court of Khusro II Aparwez (591–628) reached unparalleled peaks in sophistication and *joie de vivre*, that remained a model for the social life of courtiers and aristocrats throughout the Middle Ages. Detail of sixth-century Sassanian silvergilt jug.

Of this, the triumphant Byzantines knew nothing. They came from the far north to provinces that had slipped out of their control for up to twenty years. They were interested in more important things. 'A eunuch came to Damascus with money, and the Arabs who guarded the frontier came to him and asked for their usual subsidy. The eunuch drove them away in anger, saying: "The Emperor has hardly got money enough to pay his own army: how shall we give away his money to these dogs?"' (Theophanes, *Chronicle*.)

The struggle between Heraclius and Khusro II Aparwez was long
remembered as the Great War of Byzantine history. In the sixteenth
century a Russian patriarch still wrote that Constantinople had been
saved, though it had been caught between Persians and Avars 'like a
fish in a net'. Heraclius' rise to power and his defeat of Persia took
place in the atmosphere of a crusade: he had sailed to Constantinople
with an icon of the Virgin at the masthead; he had launched his
expeditions into Persia as a crusade to recover from the infidel the
relic of the Holy Cross, captured by the Persians in Jerusalem in 614.

These gestures have led some to describe Heraclius as the first
'medieval' ruler of Byzantium. As far as Heraclius' actual policies are
concerned, this is misleading. He was no innovator – just a basically
conservative emperor, an heir to the autocratic traditions of Justinian,
making the best of a desperate situation. Nor was Khusro II the
'infidel' of Byzantine propaganda. He ruled through a *camarilla* of
Christian servants. These Nestorian Christians had taken good care
of the precious relic of the Holy Cross: its capture and transportation
to Persia had been the victory of one party of Near Eastern Christians
over their western brethren.

Rather than bringing about any conscious changes of policy, the
Great War between Byzantium and Persia merely revealed more
sharply a state of affairs that had developed in the previous generations. The atmosphere of the Mediterranean world had changed since
the mid-sixth century. Whether we look at Byzantium, Italy,
Visigothic Spain or Gaul, we receive the same impression: much as a
traveller by train realizes, at the end of a long, slow journey, that the
landscape outside has altered – so, in the crucial generations between
the reign of Justinian and that of Heraclius, we can sense the definitive
emergence of a medieval world.

Boundaries hardened. The Byzantine empire took on the solidarity
and the splendid isolation that marked it out throughout the Middle
Ages. In the 550s Procopius still scanned the known civilized world;
Agathias, his successor, writing in the 580s, is ignorant of the western
Mediterranean, but minutely concerned with the history and religion
of Sassanian Persia. In Agathias' work, also, the division between
'Roman' and 'barbarian' widened into the chasm separating the

111 A stable universe. Archangels in the uniform of court officials, with standards of
Roman military origin (*cf.* Ill. 89). Mosaic from the Church of the Assumption,
Nicaea, Turkey.

Christian from the infidel. Procopius viewed Persia with Herodotean detachment; but for Agathias, the Persian is the *pagan* . . . 'and how can one enter into treaties with a man of different faith?' A generation before such Christian jingoism was mobilized by Heraclius, Byzantium had come to regard itself as the Christian fortress of the Near East: the Holy Cross at Jerusalem was the Ark of the Covenant, and the Byzantines regarded themselves no longer as citizens of a world-empire, but as a Chosen People ringed by hostile, pagan nations. At the other end of the Mediterranean, the same development took place, if in a different idiom: the Catholic kings of Visigothic Spain fused church and state; they ruled the far-flung cities of the Iberian peninsula through their bishops. In such a closed society, treason was equated with unbelief.

The hardening of boundaries reflects an inner rigidity. After Justinian, the Mediterranean world came to consider itself no longer as a society in which Christianity was merely the dominant religion, but as a totally Christian society. The pagans disappeared in the upper classes and even in the countryside. Once this wedge was withdrawn, the non-Christian found himself an outlaw in a unified state. The Jews felt this change immediately: in Spain, in Byzantium, in North Africa, they were subjected, for the first time, to wholesale official persecution, and to forced baptism – to compulsory 'integration' in the Christian society. The medieval idea of the 'Christian society', flanked uneasily by the ghetto, began in this period.

This change was the symptom of a rapid simplification of culture. The most important feature of the ancient world, in its Late Antique phase especially, had been the existence of a sharp boundary between aristocratic and popular culture. In the late sixth century, the boundary was all but obliterated: the culture of the Christian man in the street became, for the first time, identical with that of the élite of bishops and rulers.

In the West, the secular élite simply disappeared. Those senatorial dynasties that did not die out, to be replaced by courtiers of mixed Roman-Germanic origin, ran to bishops. Bishops were less intolerant of the classics than they claimed to be. But they were very busy men. The ancient ideal of culture had depended on an ancient style of life, in which *otium* – leisure – and a degree of alienation from politics was essential. For a brief period, from 540 to about 580, the scholar-bureaucrat, Cassiodorus, had carried the aristocratic ideal of culti-

112 The new leaders of the Byzantine town. The bishop and governor of Thessalonica, protected by St Demetrius. Early seventh-century mosaic from the Church of St Demetrius, Salonica.

vated leisure into the monastery he founded on his estate at Vivarium in southern Italy. But in the next generation, no Italian had any time for leisure: 'If our concern were with secular erudition,' wrote the Roman clergy, 'we think no one nowadays can boast much learning. Here the fury of the barbarians burns daily, now flaring up, now dying down. Our whole life is taken up in cares, and all our efforts go to beating back the war-bands that surround us.'

Even in more sheltered provinces, Spain and Gaul, a new, more strictly utilitarian ideal replaced the former standards. Basic literacy, not cultivated leisure, was the most pressing need of the bishops of the age. In the fourth century, Christ had rebuked Jerome, in a nightmare, for reading too much Cicero; in the sixth century in a similar dream, Gregory of Tours was rebuked only for spending too much time on learning shorthand. Shorthand, not a knowledge of the

113 Isidore of
Seville. From
a manuscript
of *Contra
Judaeos* (*Ms.
lat.* 13396),
probably
north-east
France, *c.* 800.

classics, was the skill most needed by the great administrator-bishops of Gaul. Even a man of culture now stood *outside* the ancient world. For Isidore of Seville (570–636), classical culture stood like a row of blue hills on the horizon: there was no telling how far apart the distant peaks were – Cicero and Augustine, Vergil and Jerome, pagan and Christian alike were revered by the seventh-century bishop, as the 'masters' of a long-dead past.

In the West, therefore, classical culture went by default. The *milieux* that had supported the classical tradition throughout the sixth century disappeared rapidly in the seventh. Even in Rome, where the clerical oligarchy fostered long memories, it was accepted that the centre of gravity of civilization had shifted back, once again, to the eastern Mediterranean. In the seventh century, travellers from the north found that the popes and their entourage whispered to each other in Greek.

The great Latin libraries, however, outlived the aristocrats who had once frequented them. Throughout the seventh and eighth centuries, Roman was the Mecca of bibliophiles from the less literate provinces; but a bishop from Spain needed to be told by an angel where he could find the text he wanted in the depths of the papal library.

Nothing shows the change of atmosphere more clearly than the fate of the book itself. The early Middle Ages was an age of lavish book-illumination – for the written word had ceased to be taken for granted in western Europe. The book itself became a holy thing. It was solemnly embellished; and reading was made easier for the uninitiated by punctuation and by the insertion of chapter-headings (both unknown in the matter-of-fact book-production of the ancient world). The great Gospel-books, the liturgical books, the carefully prepared anthologies of the sermons of the Fathers, came to stand apart, along with other holy objects, in the great basilica-churches that linked the men of the seventh and eighth centuries to their awesome, partly understood past.

Above all, those who did most to produce the books and who benefited most enthusiastically from the resources of the southern libraries, were men who had no ties with the Mediterranean. The seventh century is the great age of Irish and Northumbrian culture. In this new environment, the Late Antique legacy was completely transformed. The rudimentary ornamentation of Coptic Gospel-books suddenly spilled out into the quiet, impenetrable subtleties of Celtic illumination, whose roots lay in the prehistoric art of the La Tène period. Thus, what happened to the culture of western Europe in the seventh and eighth centuries is of interest and importance: but it is no longer part of the history of the Late Antique world.

In Byzantium, a classical élite survived. It constantly re-created itself throughout the Middle Ages. Most of our finest manuscripts of the classics were produced in medieval Constantinople. Indeed, if it were not for Byzantine courtiers and bishops of the ninth and tenth centuries onwards, we should know nothing – except from fragments in papyrus – of Plato, Euclid, Sophocles and Thucydides. The classical Greek culture that we know, is the Greek culture that continued to hold the interest of the upper classes of Constantinople throughout the Middle Ages. These men lived in their classical past so naturally that medieval Byzantium never experienced a Renaissance: Byzantines never thought that the classical past had died and so they rarely attempted, self-consciously, to have it 'reborn'. *Anakatharsis* – 'cleaning-up' – was the nearest they came to such an idea: much as an ever-present public monument is occasionally washed down and regilded in a moment of zeal.

The culture of Justinian's reign had still included areas that were opaque to Christianity. Up to the 560s, the pagan professors at Athens dominated the intellectual life of the cultivated classes. Their Christian rivals were only able to coat with a veneer of orthodoxy a Platonism that had remained firmly in pagan hands. The philosophical traditions that Greek and Syrian Christian teachers of philosophy passed on to the Arabs, in the seventh and eighth centuries, were still recognizably pagan; and the heart-searchings of many an orthodox Muslim and Catholic intellectual in the Middle Ages are a tribute to the unassimilable paganism of the Platonic Academy of Athens in the reign of Justinian.

As a result, the academic life of the age had been marked by vigorous controversy. John Philoponos, the eccentric Christian professor at Alexandria, attacked the last pagans for believing that the Heavens were divine and imperishable – and so anticipated Galileo in some of his arguments on the perishable, material nature of the stars: and he defended himself against 'fundamentalist' Christians by proving that the earth was round, and that earthquakes were caused by steam-pressure.

114 A Late Antique manuscript of the Bible: a simple, professional and matter-of-fact production, without punctuation. Leaf from the fourth-century *Codex Sinaiticus*.

115 The page has become a world of its own, full of bizarre and allegorical ornament. Detail of leaf from the *Gellone Sacramentary* (*Vat. reg. lat.* 316), written in northern France, *c.* 750.

116 The holy things. Splendid relic cases, containing the supernatural power associated with the figures on their cover were the most prized possessions of rulers a bishops in the early Middle Ages. Reliqua casket of Pepin of Aquitaine, treasure of Sainte-Foy, Conques.

THE BOOK AS A HOLY THING

117 Golden and bejewelled cover of a Gospel book, presented by Pope Gregory I to the Lombard queen, Theodolinda, *c.* 600.

118 The carved wooden reading desk of St Radegund, from her convent at Poitiers, *c.* 587.

THE CLASSICAL TRADITION
119 In public life: a Greek tragedy being performed at Constantinople in the sixth century. Detail from the ivory diptych of Anastasius.

120 In private taste: the silverware of a rich Constantinopolitan still shows scenes of classical mythology – which also provided the subjects of much exquisite poetry in the time of Justinian and his successors. Early seventh-century silver plate with Silenus and a maenad.

The culture of the civilian upper classes, also, had remained based on the classics. The poems written in the classical idiom in the sixth century were the best produced by Greeks under the Roman empire, and they were entirely pagan in mood. In the works of Procopius, we see Christianity only through the frosted glass of a classical history modelled on Herodotus and Thucydides. Wherever there were rich patrons, the gods survived in art – on Coptic textiles, in carving; and Silenus still chases the nymphs on the silverware of rich Constantinopolitans of the days of Heraclius.

The autocracy of Justinian fatally weakened the aristocratic basis of Late Antique culture: the traditional bureaucracy was weakened by personal government, and the independent life of the provincial cities, for centuries the recruiting ground of the Greek scholar-gentry, was sapped by centralization. The collapse of an independent, classical élite followed swiftly: in the late sixth century the culture of the governing class of the empire finally became indistinguishable from the Christian culture of the average man. An atmosphere of intolerance, manifested in the occasional savage punishments of Jews and of the few remaining pagans, show the norms of Roman law bending before the storms of public opinion. This period is also the golden age of Byzantine hagiography. Written in simple, yet passable Greek, these lives of saints were a triumph of 'middlebrow' culture. They were now read by all Byzantines, from the emperor downwards. The miracle-stories in the *Dialogues* of Gregory the Great are a Latin version of the same phenomenon: in them, we catch our last glimpse of the Roman Senate, curiously investigating the miraculous properties of a sarcophagus.

The new, popular culture of the late sixth century was 'medieval' in the true sense: it ran on new lines, it exploited new energies, it marked the emergence of a new, non-classical sensibility. The upper-class culture of the Late Antique world had been exclusively literary. The book and the spoken word were the only forms of culture that interested the educated man: no Late Antique bishop, for instance, so much as hints that the churches in which he preached were being set with revolutionary mosaics. By the sixth century, the literary tradition had piled up as an imposing legacy from the past. The Fathers of the Church were quarried for 'chains' – *catenae* – of quotations. In such an atmosphere, forgery throve – a sure sign that the past had become cut off from the present, and had become a timeless, flat backdrop. Sixth-century mystical writings were ascribed to Dionysius the Areopagite, a disciple of St Paul; and philosophers read the letters of Socrates – to Plotinus!

The written word had withdrawn into a shell. Music was the new idiom of the sixth century. Theological controversy hinged on the refrains of devotional chants. The Byzantine liturgy developed its dramatic form. Previously the Cross was shown in Late Antique art as a distant symbol – as a Roman trophy of victory or as a remote, star-studded sign in the sky of a mosaic vault; it was now charged with the body of the Crucified, through the pathos of the Good Friday dirges of Syria.

And, besides music – the icon. The visual image, the stylized portrait, was a concentrated and potent symbol that spoke directly to the man in the street. For the average man had lost touch with the erudite, literary symbolism that had encrusted the public life of the empire. When an emperor placed the traditional, classical winged 'genius' of Constantinople on his coins in 570, the provincials were shocked: they thought he had become a pagan; what they wanted on their coins was the simple, charged emblem of the Cross. Compared with the miscellaneous, sub-pagan attributes of the imperial office in late Roman art – the consular robes, the priestly fillet, the

181

orb with the classical winged victory – the great golden votive crowns of the Catholic kings of Visigothic Spain, in the seventh century, are compressed and moving symbols of an idea of kingship, deeply embedded in the popular imagination, without reference to the ancient Roman past. In the same way, seventh-century Byzantine emperors appealed directly to the supernatural sanction of their rule – to Christ the Pantocrator of popular devotion. In the coins of Justinian II (685–95 and 705–11), the emperor is effaced behind the great, bearded face of Christ 'the king of kings'; we are in a different world from the prancing, old-fashioned Roman horseman of the coins of Justinian I.

Icons flooded the Mediterranean world. Icons and relics – the Holy Face of Christ at Edessa, the Holy Cross at Jerusalem, the Icon of the Virgin of Constantinople – became the talismans of the empire, for they could be endowed with miraculous properties. The supernatural was 'focused' on their physical presence in the heart of the Christian cities. The art of the icon followed this trend towards focusing on a single holy object. The gay, flamboyant decoration of the fifth and early sixth centuries, the mountains and palaces made lighter than air in rainbow mosaics, disappeared. We are left face to face with a figure, isolated against the glow of golden mosaic. A glass wall stands between this new art and the floating curtains and bubbling fountains of the court-scenes of Justinian at S. Vitale.

The world of the late sixth and seventh centuries had achieved this 'focused', stable quality – at least, in men's imaginations. Like the great temples of the classical world, the cult-sites of the Dark Ages were sanctified by long memories which outlived any holy individual. They had lasted while mere men came and passed away. The new devotion was an upsurge of loyalty to holy *things*, while the enthusiasm of previous centuries had concentrated on holy *men*. In Rome and in Gaul, the relic and the martyr's grave totally ousted the living holy man in the popular imagination. No hermit ever sat at Tours in the sixth century: but the bishop and townsfolk lived under the shadow of the great basilica of St Martin, constantly aware of the presence of a man now dead for some two hundred years. It was under the protection of these relics of their saints that the cities of the Mediterranean recaptured their ancient patriotism in the crisis-ridden days of the seventh century. The history of Thessalonica, under constant siege from the Slav settlers of Macedonia, is the history of

121 Christ as 'the king of kings'. A gold *solidus* of the emperor Justinian II.

122 New symbols of kingship.
The votive crown of the
Visigothic king Recceswinth,
653–72.

the miracles of St Demetrius; that of Rome, the history of St Peter; that of Constantinople, of the Mother of God.

In a sense, we have come full circle to the days of untroubled, pagan conservatism in the age of the Antonines. Heaven and earth have settled down to a well-regulated harmony. Christianity is now the ancestral religion. If scrupulously performed, its public ceremonies were certain to avert misfortune and to secure the good favour of the supernatural. God is the remote emperor: but the towering figures of the angels, joined by long-dead heroes of the Christian religion, watch over the earth. The men of the early Middle Ages were as quietly certain as Marcus Aurelius had once been that those who held to the ways of their ancestors could expect to be cradled in the care of unseen protectors.

183

This sea-change affected the structure of society very differently in different areas. In the Byzantine empire, and especially in Asia Minor, it created a new sense of solidarity. Like the explosion of petrol-gas in a compressed piston, it was the popular fervour of the inhabitants of Constantinople, hemmed in by the Persians and Avars for almost a decade, that drove the army of Heraclius 'into the heart of godless Persia'. The high morale of medieval Constantinople, based on the sense of being the capital of an empire founded by God to last for ever, dates from this time – a time when, as often later, the Roman empire had shrunk to the walls of the city. Outside Constantinople and Asia Minor, however, Heraclius was unable to harness the new devotion to the Byzantine state. Tired and bankrupt, he returned to provinces that had not known a Christian emperor for up to twenty years. For the first time, Christian popular devotion was slipping out of the tentacles of the east Roman state.

The failure of Heraclius sealed the fate of the Roman empire, and, with it, of the bulk of the classical tradition in the Near East. From the time of Theodosius I to the reign of Justinian I, the emperors had skilfully canvassed popular opinion: by wooing the holy men, by dogmatic compromises, by pouring money into stone and mosaic, they had succeeded in making the average provincial, whatever his language, his level of culture and his theological preferences, feel that he was a 'citizen' of a single Christian empire. This was the greatest political achievement of the Late Antique world.

123 The cross without the crucified. Far left, sixth-century mosaic from Sant'Apollinare in Classe, Ravenna.

124 Christ crucified. Detail of miniature from the Syrian *Rabula Gospels*, 586.

125 Religious devotion: the eucharist. From a sixth-century Syrian plate.

It was a difficult feat. For the average man, to emerge into 'citizenship' involved being caught in a mesh of potentially contradictory loyalties. It had meant being loyal to an emperor who was technically all-powerful, but in fact unattainable; to be ruled by a governing class, part of whose culture had remained opaque to Christianity; to feel enthusiasm for a Christian empire whose ruler was, more often than not, heretical and sometimes a persecutor.

In the late sixth century, the new upsurge of popular devotion made these conflicting loyalties more difficult to contain.

In the first place, the local Christian community had grown in strength since the mid-sixth century. As a result of the reforms of Justinian, the bishop finally ousted the town councillors as the head of the cities: he rebuilt the walls; he negotiated with the tax-collectors and the barbarians. In the years of emergency at the turn of the sixth and seventh centuries, it was the patriarchs who held the great cities for the empire. In Rome, Gregory dissolved the estates of the Church in a desperate bid to keep the life of Rome going. John the Almsgiver did exactly the same in Alexandria from 610 to 617: during his patriarchate, the city became a Byzantine welfare state in miniature, with maternity hospitals, medical facilities and food rationing, provided from the vast revenue of the patriarch. These men saved the great cities of the Mediterranean world for the empire, if only for a moment. But it was they, not the governors sent out from Constantinople, who now represented the towns. Under the Arabs, the

185

local patriarchs of Alexandria maintained the life of Alexandria just as effectively as John had done, under Heraclius; their activities showed that the average Christian had found leadership and protection nearer home, irrespective of his rulers.

It was more than a social evolution. The new popular devotion marked the resurgence of an ancient theme – the ideal of a totally religious culture. This did not happen earlier. The east Roman state had maintained a sub-pagan façade in most aspects of its public life; large areas of education and public life were frankly 'secular'. Its governors were reared on the literature of the old gods: a Greek-style theatre, for instance, has recently been discovered from sixth-century Alexandria. Christian opinion was increasingly impatient with these exotic trappings. It was not to be impatient for much longer. Paradoxically, the arrival of the Arab armies completed the Christianization of the public life of the cities of the Near East. The last vestige of a secular culture based on the Greek classics disappeared. Christian clergymen eventually passed Aristotle, Plato and Galen on to the Arabs; but in the medieval Near East, Christian and Muslim alike chose to remain ignorant of Homer, of Thucydides, of Sophocles. It was the end of a millennium of literary culture. In the words of the great new chant to the Virgin: 'The many-tongued rhetors have fallen silent as fishes' throughout the Near East.

Under Muslim rule, the new style of Christian culture, that had been prepared in the later sixth century, came to harden round the Christian populations of the Near East. It preserved them up to modern times.

In this new culture, a man was defined by his religion alone. He did not owe allegiance to a state; he belonged to a religious community. His culture was preserved for him by his religious leaders; thus Coptic and Syriac have survived up to modern times, but only as 'sacred' languages. Such a development had been anticipated in Persian-dominated Mesopotamia: there, the Jews and the Nestorian Christians had always formed distinct groups, responsible to the government through their religious leaders. Both among the rabbis and among the Nestorian scholars of Nisibis, there was no such thing as an independent 'secular' culture: all learning was subordinated to the elaboration of a religious tradition. But even in the Byzantine empire, the provincial bishops of the late sixth century were moving in the same direction. John the Almsgiver, sitting outside his palace and

126 The new pathos: the death of Jacob. Acute expression of grief was a hallmark of Byzantine ascetic piety. Miniature from the sixth-century *Vienna Genesis*.

settling the disputes of the city of Alexandria according to the Law of God, is a direct anticipation of the Muslim *cadi*.

The arrival of the Arabs merely cut the last threads that had bound the provincials of the Near East to the Roman empire. In the Arab empire nobody was a 'citizen' in the classical sense. This was the final victory of the idea of the religious community over the classical idea of the state. The Muslims were slaves of Allah and the others were *dhimmis* – protected groups, defined entirely in terms of their religious allegiances: Christians, Jews, Zoroastrians. The bishops who negotiated with the Muslim generals in the name of their towns during the lightning conquests of the 640s and 650s were confirmed for a thousand years to come in the position they had imperceptibly won for themselves since the reign of Justinian.

The ancient world had died in the imagination of the inhabitants of the eastern Mediterranean. Popular legend was aware of this. When John the Almsgiver sailed from Alexandria to ask the emperor for help, he was told in a dream not to waste his time: 'God is always close at hand; but the emperor is far, far away. . . .'

187

الفرس بالماء

XV MUHAMMAD AND THE RISE OF ISLAM, 610–632

Eight hundred miles to the south of the Byzantine frontier, in Mecca, a town of the Hijaz, a man reaching middle age after a mediocre career as a merchant had taken to wandering disconsolately among the grim hill-tops outside the town. In 610, this man, Muhammad, began to see visions. He recited these in verse form to make up his *Qur'an*, his 'recitation'. On the strength of these experiences, he grouped a community round himself – the *'Umma*, the 'people of Allah'. Within twenty years, Muhammad and his *'Umma* were established as the rulers of Mecca and the neighbouring Medina, and as the dominant party in the Arabian peninsula.

The preaching of Muhammad and the consequent rise of a new religious grouping of the Arab world – the religion of Islam – was the last, most rapid crisis in the religious history of the Late Antique period.

We know just enough about the Hijaz in the early seventh century to see how this sudden detonation fitted into the culture of the Near East. The inhabitants of Mecca and Medina were far from being primitive Beduin. The towns had grown rapidly through trade and were supported by settled agriculture. They were ruled by oligarchies, who had suddenly found themselves the merchant-princes of the seventh-century Near East. As we have seen, the caravans of the Meccan merchant-adventurers had come to permeate Byzantium and Persia: Muhammad himself had once made the trek to Syria. The wives of these men performed their toilet like Persian ladies, before polished bronze mirrors imported from China. In Medina, Jewish settlements linked the Arabs to the religious life of Jerusalem and Nisibis. To the south, in the more sophisticated Yemen, the imperialism of the negus of Ethiopia had brought a sub-Coptic style of Christianity to within two hundred miles of Mecca. Even the *Ka'aba* itself was rebuilt, in about 600, on the model of an Ethiopian church; it may have included icons of the Virgin in its decoration.

189

127 Arab horseman in a tenth-century pen drawing.

Yet for all these foreign contacts, Mecca kept out of the maelstrom of Near Eastern civilization. Its elder statesmen pursued a canny policy of neutrality. Its inhabitants held aloof from Christians, Jews and Persians. They were still held back by the fully developed style of life which they shared with the nomadic Beduin. They were as proud of it as they were of the resources of their own language – a language formed by epic poetry, and ideally suited to a tribal environment; it was a style of life hallowed by custom and by the lack of any viable alternative for that harsh land.

Muhammad cut the inhabitants of the Hijaz loose from the ties of tribal custom and threw them into the Fertile Crescent. His message developed as a protest against the Beduin way of life. Seldom has a religion made so explicit the sanctions by which a man should rule his life as did Islam; and seldom has it come into such immediate and lasting conflict with a fully articulated alternative rule of life, as did Islam with the tribal values of the Arab world.

The Arab tribal ideal had been wholeheartedly extrovert. A man was held rigidly to the obligations of his tribe. His conduct was guided by the fear of incurring shame through lapses in public behaviour, by the desire to win praise from his fellows, by the need to uphold the nobility of his ancestry by spectacular deeds of generosity, of courage, by exacting swift revenge, and by tenacious observance of a network of obligations. To follow this way of life was to 'be a man'.

In direct contrast to this communal ideal, the Muslim was an atom. Every tie of human society, so Muhammad believed, would vanish like dust at the Last Judgment. Then, men would stand in awesome loneliness, without fellow tribesmen, without protectors, even without relatives. In this life, the Muslim was to rule himself, not by maintaining a brittle 'face' against the outside world of his fellow tribesmen, but by a personal, intimate 'fear', driven into his heart by the thought of the Judgment of Allah. 'Shame' is no longer the bitter wound inflicted on a man by tribal opinion; it is the intimate anxiety of exposure at the Last Day. Even the Muslim taboo on wine was connected less with the wish to avoid drunkenness, than with a shrewd concern to remove a traditional aid to motivation. For it was widely believed that, in his cups, the Arab gentleman could 'feel his blood speak'. Through wine, he became mindful of the deeds of his ancestors; he felt able to live up to an ancient style of life – lavish, polished and grandiloquent (not unlike that of the heroes of Homer or the *cortezia* of a medieval Provençal baron). The Muslim could not tolerate such easy spontaneity: not wine and warm memories of the past, but the chill dread of the Last Judgment, must spur on a man.

The immediate sources of the guiding ideas of Muhammad are easy to see. Whatever he may have thought about the Christian Church, the Muslim guided his conduct by exactly the same considerations as did any Christian or Jew throughout the Fertile Crescent. He, too, was a 'God-fearer'. He, too, had faced the terrible choice of the Last Judgment, infallibly revealed to him in a Sacred Book. He, too, must think on it day and night. The Syrian hermit who 'wept like a father mourning his dead child' at the thought of the Last Judgment was venerated because he summed up an ideal of behaviour to which the populations of the Near East subscribed without question – even if the majority prudently avoided exposing themselves to acting on it. Muhammad imposed this ideal on all his Arab followers. In so doing, he brought the Arabs into civilization as it was known in the seventh-century Near East.

It was a stroke of genius on the part of Muhammad to turn this essentially foreign message into a principle on which the conflict-ridden society of the Hijaz could reorganize itself. He was called upon to cure the *malaise* of an 'emergent' society. In the towns, the tribal style of life was losing its hold on the *nouveaux riches* of the merchant-dynasties. Private and public standards of behaviour were being torn apart by new wealth, new opportunities and new ideas. Faced by this situation, Muhammad cut the knot of conflicting values. He reduced his followers to the loneliness of atoms in the face of Allah: but in order to bind them together as a new 'people' – the *'Umma*. Within the fold of the *'Umma*, the abrasive tensions of tribal life were mercifully suspended. Under Muhammad as a religious leader, peace came to towns whose magnificent style of life had plainly outstripped the rough ethics of the desert, with murderous results. As the inhabitants of Medina said: 'Allah has sent us a prophet who will make peace between us.' It was as an arbitrator, backed by a core of devoted fighting-men, that Muhammad rose to power in Arabia. Driven from Mecca, in 622, by traditionalist opinion, he and his *'Umma* imposed peace on the feuding parties of Medina. When he returned in triumph to Mecca in 630, Muhammad set about transforming the commercial influence of the city, based on the trade fair round the sanctuary of the *Ka'aba*, into a religious empire. He struck up alliances between the Beduin tribes and the new 'super-tribe', his *'Umma*. When he died in 632, Muhammad had turned the whole Arabian peninsula into a zone of truce: Islam, it was said, had come 'to make their hearts one'.

For the Arabs, Muhammad had brought peace, but for the rest of the Near East – a sword. Islam had suspended the traditional feuding among the Beduin tribes, who were now nominally Muslims. Their ancient aggression had to find another outlet: internal feuds were rapidly transmuted into the standing feud between the *'Umma* and the unbeliever. A year after the last Bedouin recalcitrants were coerced into the Islamic confederacy, the Muslim generals declared the Holy War against Byzantine Syria. 'It was not for love of Heaven that you fought there,' wrote a Beduin poet, 'but for love of bread and dates.' The conquest of the Byzantine and Persian empires was the price which others had to pay for the success of the *pax Islamica* among the Arabs.

Thus, at just the moment when (as we have seen) the Arab tribes along the frontiers of Byzantium and Persia had to face the threat of ostracism, and consequent proletarization, the message of Muhammad filled up the chasm between the Arabs and their contemptuous neighbours, the civilized populations of the Fertile Crescent. The ethical teachings of Islam made the Arab Muslim the equal of the 'God-fearing' Jew and Christian. The *Qur'an* provided the illiterate Arab tribesmen with the basis of a literary culture that imitated, and would soon rival, the Bible of the Christian monk and the *Torah* of the rabbi.

More immediately, the foundation of the Islamic community placed an amazing generation of young men – notably, the first califs, Abu Bekr (632–34) and Umar (634–44) – in control of the Beduin world. This core of devoted 'true believers' provided the under-Islamized Beduin raiding-parties with an unequalled High Command. The radicalism of the early Muslims extended to the art of war. The Muslim supporters of Muhammad had introduced the technology of fortification and siege warfare into the Hijaz. After Muhammad's death, the Muslim core of the Beduin armies faced the Byzantines and Persians as equals in the art of armoured cavalry-warfare. They used the traditional mobility of the Beduin, based on the camel; the camel carried a nucleus of fully equipped soldiers, at baffling speed, to all points along the Byzantine frontiers, as aeroplanes would now carry paratroops.

Above all, the Muslim generals came as conquerors, not as tribal raiders. The career of Muhammad, who had created a religious empire in Arabia almost exclusively through negotiation, provided the first califs with precedents for acute diplomacy. In the first decades of their conquests, the Arabs gained quite as much by treaty as by the sword: key cities, such as Damascus and Alexandria, fell because the Muslim High Command was instantly prepared to offer generous terms – protection and toleration in return for a fixed tribute.

Hence the awesome and baffling quality of the arrival of the first Muslim armies in the provinces of the Byzantine empire – they were something a little more than the accustomed Beduin. When the patriarch of Jerusalem went out to meet his conquerors in 638, he found himself confronted with a tiny band of men like monks on horseback: the Muslim generals told him that they had come as pilgrims to the Holy Places. This was the last straw: 'Behold the abomination of desolation standing in the place where it should not stand.' In this sub-Christian guise the Arabs had found a place in the sun. As an Arab ambassador told the shah of Persia:

'Once the Arabs were a wretched race, whom you could tread under foot with impunity. We were reduced to eating dogs and lizards. But, for our glory, God has raised up a prophet among us. . . .'

128 Islam, even more than Christianity, was a religion of the book; and the good Muslim (like the medieval monk) was a devout reader and copier of its holy text. *Qu'ran* – 'recitation' – is derived from the solemn devotional recitation of the holy scriptures by the Syrian monks. Leaf from an Egypto-Arabic *Qu'ran*: Kufic script on parchment, eighth–ninth century.

The victories of the Arab armies created a political vacuum in the Near East. The Byzantines were routed at the battle of the Yarmuk in 636: Antioch fell in 637; Alexandria in 642; Carthage in 698. The Persian army put up a more stubborn resistance; but after the battle of Qadesiya in 637, the Sassanian state crumbled. None of the traditional powers were in a position to win back what they had lost in these lightning campaigns. Only Byzantium survived with its capital and administration intact. Yet a second Heraclius never came. Hence an uneasy stillness descended on the eastern Mediterranean. Even under Arab rule, Syria and Egypt remained in close contact with the rest of the world throughout the seventh century: Italian pilgrims travelled comfortably to Jerusalem, Alexandrian papyrus still stocked the chancery of the popes. But no Christian army ever returned to these eastern shores until the time of the Crusades.

Having excluded all possible rivals, the Arabs set about ruling a world empire with remarkable astuteness, eclecticism and a tolerance based on an unshakable sense of their own superiority: 'The finest of all people are the Arabs, and among the Arabs, the tribe of Mudar, and among that tribe, the clan of Ya'sur, and among that clan, the family of Ghani . . . and among the Ghani, I am the finest man. Hence, I am the finest of all mankind.'

Needless to say, such sentiments are not to be found in the *Qur'an*. But they formed the backbone of the Arab empire in its first century – the century of the Umayyad califs of Damascus. For the Umayyad empire was an undisguised Arab supremacy, based on the partially Islamized warrior-aristocracy of the Arab tribes. The Beduin way of life of the Arab aristocracy, though castigated by Muhammad, saved Islam. It was the chieftains of the Beduin tribes who created the Arab war-machine with their rude followers, and it was the style of life of this warrior-aristocracy – and not the sheltered piety of the core of devout Muslims – that held the empire together.

In the first place, it saved the Arab conquerors from losing their identity in the overwhelming mass of their conquered populations. Unregenerate, utterly self-confident and fully articulate, the Beduin style of living 'like a man', lightly Islamized, absorbed and remodelled the educated classes of the early medieval Near East. The style of life

129 Late Antiquity surviving. A mosaic from the Umayyad mosque at Damascus, built in 706–15 to out-do the Byzantine monuments in the Holy Land.

of the Arab conquerors, above all the intricate poetic literature that the Arabs had brought fully formed from the desert, proved infectious. Even non-Muslims quickly absorbed Arab culture. The Christians of southern Spain, for instance, were called 'Mozarabic' because, though Christians, they nevertheless 'wished to be like Arabs'. 'Many of my co-religionists', wrote a ninth-century bishop of Cordova, 'read verses and fairy-tales of the Arabs, and study the works of Muhammadan philosophers and theologians, not in order to refute them, but to learn to express themselves in the Arab language more correctly and more elegantly.'

In the first century of their empire, the Arabs ruled from the edge of the desert. They turned the political map of the Near East inside-out. Damascus, the watchpost of the east Roman defences towards the desert, became the capital of the Arab califs in their watch on the east Romans. The desert fortresses of Diocletian became the hunting lodges of Arab princes; while the once peaceful city of Antioch, whose villas these forts had protected, became an armed camp from which the Arab armies issued, every year, to spread devastation along the coast and up the valleys of Asia Minor.

To the Arab supremacy, the populations that lay behind their advancing armies were not even conquered territories in the strict sense. For they were hardly occupied. They were treated as the rich neighbours of the Arabs who paid protection-money to the 'Umma, to the Muslims, in return for military defence and as a sort of standing fine for not having embraced Islam. Hence the almost total *laissez-faire* of the seventh-century Arabs. The tax-machines of Syria, Egypt and Persia were encouraged to work smoothly in order to provide the Muslims with pensions. Thus maintained in unparalleled affluence, the Arab governing class fought out its bitter battles for power according to the laws of Beduin behaviour, in the hermetically sealed environments of the great garrison-cities – Kufa and Basra, on the edge of the desert facing Persian Mesopotamia, and Al-Fostāt, in Egypt. For them, the conquered provinces were 'a garden protected by our spears'.

This was an exact description of the Near East in the seventh and eighth centuries. Populations formed by the developments of the late ancient world found their life continuing, *in vacuo*, with, if anything, increased comfort and self-confidence. The grain-levies from Egypt to Constantinople were abolished. A vast Common

Market in trade and craftsmanship came into being: for the first time, Copt and Persian could work side by side in producing a magnificent building such as the palace at M'Shatta. After the débâcle of Khusro II Aparwez, firm government and the renewal of irrigation works returned to Mesopotamia – notably during the governorship of Al-Hajjaj (692–724), a former schoolteacher and one of the greatest administrators in medieval history. As the storm of the Arab armies rolled over the horizon, the populations of the Near East sat back to enjoy the sunshine.

While the Arab fleet hemmed in Constantinople, local masons and mosaic-workers were creating, in the Dome of the Rock at Jerusalem and in the Great Mosque of Damascus, buildings as magnificent as ever Justinian I had lavished on the province. In Qusair 'Amra, Syrian painters of the early eighth century decorated the palace of an Arab gentleman with frescoes that are the last pure and untroubled efflorescence of Hellenistic grace. Far away from the care-worn world of the northern Mediterranean, Syrian abbots were quietly reading Plato and Aristotle, and the last Father of the Byzantine Church, St John Damascene, summed up the orthodox tradition of past centuries in the shelter of the court of the califs – where he held a financial post first occupied by his great-grandfather under the emperor Heraclius.

By 800, the traditions formed in the Late Antique period in the various countries of the Mediterranean had diverged sharply. Byzantium emerged from the crisis of the Arab conquests to find that its classical legacy had shrunk to the walls of Constantinople. The idea of the Roman empire was still very much alive in the streets of the city, in the majestic ceremonial of the imperial processions; and a small circle of clerics and courtiers maintained, at Constantinople, standards of culture that had once been available to the inhabitants of any considerable Greek town in the later Roman empire. In Rome, the ancient glory still haunted the city in an attenuated, clerical form. Far to the north, at the court of Charlemagne, a circle of cosmopolitan clergymen – many of whom, being Irish or northern Englishmen of Irish education, came from countries that had never even known Roman rule – nevertheless struck up a passable imitation of the courtly literati of the days of Ausonius and Sidonius Apollinaris.

In Byzantium and the West, therefore, the bases of civilization either had become impoverished or had had to be painfully resurrected by a small élite in an alien environment. Throughout the Arab empire, by contrast, these Late Antique forms had continued a buoyant life. In the eighth- and ninth-century Near East, this rich life forced itself upwards to the notice of the Arab governing classes. But when this happened, the traditions of Greece and Rome, of the Mediterranean seaboard, had to compete with those of the Sassanian empire, of eastern Mesopotamia and the great land-mass of the Iranian plateau, whose sprawling eastern lands were known to the Arabs as Khurasan.

The Arab aristocracy could not maintain its hold on the government indefinitely, for the Arab supremacy was undermined by Islam itself. Islam made all its converts equal, whatever their racial origin. It opened the floodgates to the gifted or the ambitious non-Arab. As Muslims, Syrians and Persians became the pillars of Islamic civilization: they came to be the administrators, the lawyers, the theologians, even, within only a century, the professors of Arab poetry. Medieval Islam was very largely the creation of Muslim non-Arabs.

Thus, the Arab empire of the eighth and ninth centuries had to face a similar problem to that of the Roman empire in the third century: the sudden erosion of a proud traditional oligarchy, largely in the interests of strong government. Just as the narrow certainties of the traditional Greco-Roman aristocracy were swamped by the diffused and energetic patriotism of the Roman provincials in the fourth century, so the non-Arab Muslims, in the eighth century, came to the rescue of the Arab empire. As a result, the culture of the ruling class widened its franchise: much as the existence of new avenues to power, in the fourth and fifth centuries, fostered the spread of Latin and Greek culture, so – on a far wider scale – the absorption of Arabic, and of an Arab style of life, opened the court to the provincials of the Near East. Just as, in the Late Antique period, Syrians, Egyptians and Cappadocians, in reading their Homer, took into their lives ideals of behaviour modelled on the exotic adventures of Mycenaean chieftains, so, from Cordova to Samarkand, educated men, of widely different origins and of resolutely urban tastes, spoke classical Arabic and claimed to be acting as true sons of the tents. But whereas, in the Roman empire of the fourth and fifth centuries, the traditional culture of the governing classes remained dominant, remained the giver into whose benefits backward provinces were proud to emerge, in the Arab empire of the eighth century a thousand years of civilization found its voice again,

130 The triumph of the East. The late classical heads are already almost engulfed in
the exuberant ornamentation that is derived directly from Persian models. It was this
revival of Persian tastes and artistic traditions, rather than any original antipathy on
the part of the Muslims, that smothered the Late Antique forms of representational
art. Ceiling rosette from Khirbat al-Mafjar.

after a hiatus of Beduin rule, with the rise to power of the Muslim non-Arabs.

Thus the late seventh and the early eighth centuries, and not the age of the first Arab conquests, are the true turning-point in the history of Europe and the Near East. This happened first in a prolonged confrontation with Byzantium. In the last decades of the seventh century, the boundaries between the Christian and the Muslim worlds hardened notably. In 680/1, the sixth Oecumenical Council at Constantinople treated the patriarchates of Antioch, Jerusalem and Alexandria as no longer part of the Byzantine Christian world. In 695, the first fully Arabic coins were minted. In 699, Greek was replaced by Arabic in the chancery at Damascus. Between 706 and 714, the Great Mosque at Damascus was built, to eclipse the tantalizing magnificence of the imperial churches of Syria and Palestine. The eastern Mediterranean began to take on its Islamic face.

The califs of Damascus staked their authority on this confrontation with the Byzantine empire – the *Rūm*. But Constantinople held firm: the great naval expeditions of 677 and 717 were beaten back from under the walls of the city. There is no doubt that, at that time, Byzantium saved Europe: but, in beating back the Muslims of Syria, the Byzantine emperors unwittingly lost the Near East forever.

For, having lost its gamble in the Mediterranean, the Umayyad califate at Damascus was no longer able to control the discontented Muslims of Mesopotamia and of Persia proper (Khurasan). Umayyad rule was replaced by a dynasty supported by Islamized Persians – the Abbasid dynasty. The revolt began in Iran in 750; its outcome was sealed by the foundation of Baghdad in 762. This was the end of the Arab supremacy. As a Muslim wrote in the next century: 'The Umayyad dynasty was an Arab empire; the Abbasid dynasty, a Persian empire.'

Thus, in the end, it was the traditions of Khusro I Anoshirwan which won over those of Justinian I. The califs of Damascus had planted the Arab empire on less fertile soil than they thought. They had reckoned without the hardening of Christian communal feeling in Egypt and Syria from the time of Justinian onwards. Syrians and Copts had become used to maintaining their identity in the face of unsympathetic governments. As subjects of the Umayyads they stood aloof. The Islamic state of the Umayyads was cramped by the massive, unabsorbable traditions of the eastern Mediterranean seaboard.

To the east, however, Arab rule was always more firmly established. The garrison-cities of Kufa and Basra were new foundations, undwarfed by an alien past. And in Mesopotamia and Persia, the Muslim ruling class was able to draw on a vast reservoir of eager recruits. For the Arabs had swallowed the Sassanian empire whole. There was no surviving state to which a Persian could look, as the Christians of the Mediterranean cities still looked to Byzantium. In parts of the Iranian plateau, Zoroastrianism continued. Vigorous Zoroastrian polemic in the ninth century, for instance, gave birth to the bitter legend that troubled medieval and Renaissance Christendom: the legend of the three impostors – Moses, Christ and Muhammad (a wry comment, from distant Persia, on the three forces that most preoccupied Mediterranean men in our period!). But the whole tendency of the late Sassanian empire had been to identify religion and society: they were 'twin brothers'. The Persians, therefore, had never developed that fierce sense of a religious identity that had kept the Umayyads at arm's length among the Christians of the Mediterranean seaboard. Khusro I had taught the *dekkans*, the courtier-gentlemen of Persia, to look to a strong ruler in Mesopotamia. Under the Arabs, the *dekkans* promptly made themselves indispensable. They set about quietly storming the governing class of the Arab empire. By the middle of the eighth century, they had emerged as the backbone of the new Islamic state. It was their empire again: and, now in perfect Arabic, they poured scorn on the refractory Beduin who had dared to elevate the ways of the desert over the ordered majesty of the throne of the Khusros.

Thus, in the century following the foundation of Baghdad, especially in the reign of Harun al-Rashid (788–809) and his successors, a world that had never lost touch with its Late Antique roots enjoyed a final efflorescence in its last, Muslim and Arabic-speaking transformation.

Baghdad was only thirty-five miles from the empty halls of Ctesiphon. The calif was elevated above the Arab warriors by a Sassanian court ceremonial. His bureaucrats aimed to recover the fairy-tale affluence of the days of Khusro II Aparwez. Their style of culture, also, relived the courtly ethos first created round Khusro I Anoshirwan: an Arab gentleman of the ninth century was still expected to know 'to which of his vassals Ardashir [the founder of the Sassanian empire] had given the name of king'.

The first, decisive contact of the Arabs with Greek philosophy followed channels first cut in the sixth century. Not direct contact with Byzantium, but the long-enduring Hellenism of the Syriac-speaking clergy of Mesopotamia fed the courtiers of Harun al-Rashid with translations of Plato, Aristotle and Galen, just as they had formerly ministered to the curiosity of Khusro I Anoshirwan.

Mesopotamia regained a central position that it had lost since the days of Alexander the Great. Baghdad, with its circular city wall, owed nothing to the great cities of the Roman empire: it was an avatar of the round cities of Assyria and central Asia. The Mediterranean cities declined as the great caravans by-passed them, bringing trade by camel along the oceans of sand that stretched from the Sahara to the Gobi Desert. In North Africa and Syria, the villages that had sent their oil and grain across the sea to Rome and Constantinople disappeared into the sand. The Mediterranean coast, from being the heart of the civilized world, imperceptibly diminished in significance, as the numbed extremity of a great Eurasian empire.

For the new commercial opportunities were in Persian hands. And, in Persian hands, the eternal lure of Further Asia reasserted itself, as in the early Sassanian period. The mosque and the fire temple could be seen beside the market-places of Lohang and Canton. Chinese prisoners of war from central Asia brought the art of paper-making to Baghdad in 751. Sinbad the Sailor would not have considered the Mediterranean worth his trouble: for the wealth and interests of the Abbasid empire poured eastwards, down the Tigris and Euphrates, to the sea route that linked Basra directly with Canton.

The eastward pull of the vast mass of Persia in the Islamic empire was the salvation of Europe. It was not the Greek fire of the Byzantine navy outside Constantinople in 717, nor the Frankish cavalry of Charles Martel at Tours in 732, that brought the Arab war-machine to a halt. It was the foundation of Baghdad. With the establishment of the Abbasid califate, the slow-moving ideals of an organized and expensive imperial administration replaced the fearful mobility of the Beduin armies. In the new civilian world, the soldier was as much out of place as he had been among the otiose aristocrats of the fourth-century West. The bloodsucking relationships of the Holy War, by which the early Arabs had first impinged on the outside world, gave way to a meticulous diplomacy modelled on the protocol of the Persian *ancien régime*. At the court of the califs, the world appeared to revolve like clockwork round Baghdad, as in the dreamlike ceremonial of the king of kings. Just before he was crowned Roman emperor of the West in 800, Charlemagne received from Harun al-Rashid a great cloak and a pet elephant called Abul Abaz. Little did the Frankish monarch know it, but in this gift the calif had merely repeated the time-honoured gesture of Khusro I Anoshirwan when, at the great Spring festival, the king of kings had lavished gifts of animals and cast-off clothing on his humble servants.

In the western imagination, the Islamic empire stands as the quintessence of an oriental power. Islam owed this crucial orientation neither to Muhammad nor to the adaptable conquerors of the seventh century, but to the massive resurgence of eastern, Persian traditions in the eighth and ninth centuries.

The division between East and West, which had been blurred throughout the Late Antique period by the confrontation of Byzantium and Persia along the Fertile Crescent, came to rest along the shores of the Mediterranean itself. The Muslim world turned its back on its poor Christian neighbours across the sea. The cultivated man drew his language from the desert, and the style of his culture from eastern Mesopotamia. In the more stable world created by this vast shift of the balance of culture, western Europe could create an identity of its own. But the student of Late Antiquity, who realizes how much European culture owes to the fruitful interchange between the populations of the Fertile Crescent, open at one end to an empire based on the sea and, at the other, to the Iranian plateau, can estimate the cost of the chasm that yawned across the Mediterranean throughout the Middle Ages.

BRITAIN

Rhine
Cologne
Trier • Mainz
Moselle ALAMANNI
Strasbourg Danube

GAUL Sirmium
Saône PANNONIA
Tours• Stridon?
Milan DALMATIA Naissus
Lyons• Po Adrianople
Vienne Pavia Constanti
Bordeaux Ravenna MACEDONIA STRAIT
Rhône DOBRUDJA
Toulouse Marseilles Lérins Thessalonica MARMAR
Narbonne MILVIAN BRIDGE Smyrn
Ostia Rome Ephe
CAMPANIA N
Nola
CR
Vivarium
SICILY
Piazza Armerina
Cordova
Seville Hippo Regius MEDITERRAN
Ceuta Carthage
Thagaste
Timgad Cyrer
Ptolemais
AFRICA Lepcis Magna CYR

204

SOGHDIA

OXUS

Kabul •

CASPIAN SEA

• Gurgan
GURGAN

ARMENIA

K SEA

a CAPPADOCIA
• Nyssa
• Caesarea
Nazianzus
IA

Tarsus
CILICIA

CYPRUS

SEA

dria

ZAGROS MTNS.

Tigris

MESOPOTAMIA
• Nisibis
• Edessa
HARRAN
MTNS.
• Dura-Europos

Antioch
SYRIA
• Palmyra

• Damascus

Tyre

• Gaza

NEGEV
DESERT

EGYPT
yrhynchus •

• Dastgard
• Beit Selok (Kerkuk)
• Holwan
Ctesiphon
Baghdad •

Euphrates

Naqsh-i-Rustam

Persepolis
• Istakhr

FARS

• Basra
PERSIAN GULF

Kufa • Hira • Qadesiya

HIJAZ
• Medina

YEMEN

Tabennisi
Atripe •• Thebes
Nag-Hammadi
THEBAID

NUBIA

Nile

RED

SEA

• Mecca

Tarsus •
Callinicum •

• Antioch
Euphrates

• Apamea

SYRIA
Palmyra •
• Baalbek

• Damascus

• Tyre
• Ptolemais
Caesarea • Bostra
yarmuk • Gerasa
Jerusalem • • M'Shatta
• Bethlehem
• Gaza

205

CHRONOLOGY *Significant events are marked with an asterisk*

150	175	200	225	250	275	300

MARCUS AURELIUS 161⟵⟶180   SEPTIMIUS SEVERUS 193⟵⟶211   AURELIAN 270–275   DIOCLETIAN 284⟵⟶305   CONSTAN… 306⟵

BRITAIN
GAUL & SPAIN

260–268
POSTUMUS
in Gaul

258–268
GALLIENUS defends Italy

244⟵⟶270
PLOTINUS teaches
in Rome

*271 AURELIAN
builds walls of
Rome

✖ 312 Mil…
Bridge
Conversio…
of Constan…

ITALY & AFRICA

248–258
CYPRIAN bishop
of Carthage

240⟵⟶ LACTANTIUS ⟶320…

BALKANS, GREECE & ASIA MINOR

251 Defeat and death of DECIUS
269 CLAUDIUS defeats Goths

257 Edict against Christians

*302 Great
Persecution

*168 CELSUS' *True Doctrine*
against the Christians

GALEN
129⟵⟶199

DEXIPPUS OF ATHENS
fl. 253⟵⟶276

AELIUS ARISTIDES
118⟵⟶180

DIO CASSIUS
writes 229* *Roman History*

*268 Heruls raid Athens

324
Foundation
of Constanti…

SYRIA & PALESTINE

ZENOBIA OF PALMYRA
267–270 273 AURELIAN in East
IAMBLICHUS

SHAPUR I captures Antioch *260⟵

EUSEBIUS OF CAESAREA

263⟵

PORPHYRY
232⟵⟶303

ST ANTHONY

ORIGEN OF ALEXANDRIA c. 250⟵

c. 185⟵⟶254
writes *248 *Against Celsus*

*269 ST ANTHONY becomes a hermit

PLOTINUS
205⟵⟶270

ARIUS
250⟵

ATHANASIUS
296⟵

PACHOMIUS
290⟵
founds monastery *3…
at Tabennisi

EGYPT, PERSIA & ARABIA

MANI
216⟵⟶277

296 GALERIUS defeats Pe…

*224
Revolt
of
Fars

SHAPUR
240⟵⟶272

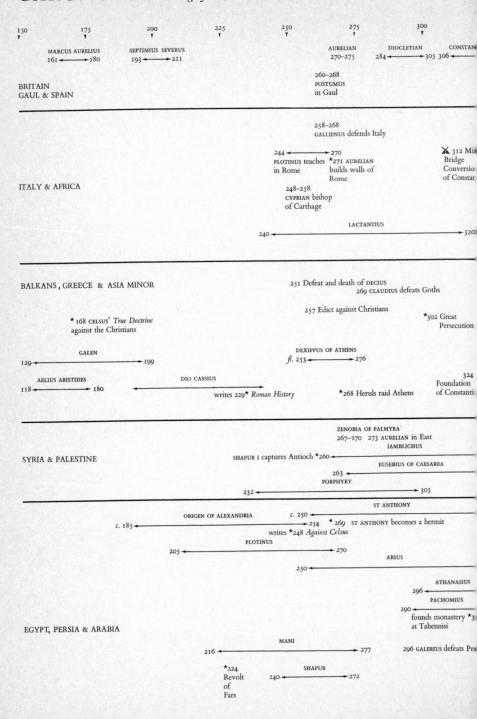

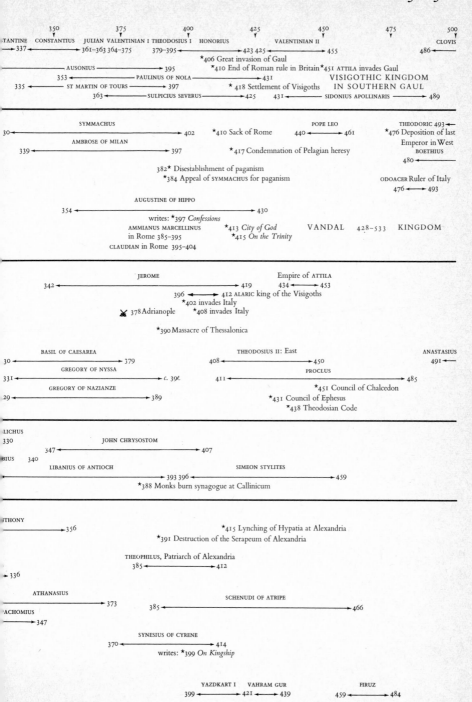

350   375   400   425   450   475   500

STANTINE CONSTANTIUS JULIAN VALENTINIAN I THEODOSIUS I HONORIUS VALENTINIAN II CLOVIS
→337← 361–363 364–375 379–395 423 425 455 486←

*406 Great invasion of Gaul
AUSONIUS →395 *410 End of Roman rule in Britain *451 ATTILA invades Gaul
353← PAULINUS OF NOLA →431 VISIGOTHIC KINGDOM
335← ST MARTIN OF TOURS →397 *418 Settlement of Visigoths IN SOUTHERN GAUL
363← SULPICIUS SEVERUS →425 431← SIDONIUS APOLLINARIS →489

SYMMACHUS POPE LEO THEODORIC 493←
30← →402 *410 Sack of Rome 440← →461 *476 Deposition of last
AMBROSE OF MILAN Emperor in West
339← →397 *417 Condemnation of Pelagian heresy BOETHIUS
480←

382* Disestablishment of paganism
*384 Appeal of SYMMACHUS for paganism ODOACER Ruler of Italy
476← →493

AUGUSTINE OF HIPPO
354← →430
writes: *397 Confessions
AMMIANUS MARCELLINUS *413 City of God VANDAL 428–533 KINGDOM
in Rome 385–395 *415 On the Trinity
CLAUDIAN in Rome 395–404

JEROME Empire of ATTILA
342← →419 434← →453
396← 412 ALARIC king of the Visigoths
*402 invades Italy
✗ 378 Adrianople *408 invades Italy
*390 Massacre of Thessalonica

BASIL OF CAESAREA THEODOSIUS II: East ANASTASIUS
30← →379 408← →450 491←
GREGORY OF NYSSA PROCLUS
331← c. 396 411← →485
GREGORY OF NAZIANZE *451 Council of Chalcedon
29← →389 *431 Council of Ephesus
*438 Theodosian Code

LICHUS
330 JOHN CHRYSOSTOM
347← →407
BIUS 340
LIBANIUS OF ANTIOCH SIMEON STYLITES
→393 396← →459
*388 Monks burn synagogue at Callinicum

ITHONY *415 Lynching of Hypatia at Alexandria
→356 *391 Destruction of the Serapeum of Alexandria

THEOPHILUS, Patriarch of Alexandria
385← →412
→336

ATHANASIUS SCHENUDI OF ATRIPE
→373 385← →466
ACHOMIUS
→347

SYNESIUS OF CYRENE
370← →414
writes: *399 On Kingship

YAZDKART I VAHRAM GUR FIRUZ
399← →421 →439 459← →484

CHRONOLOGY

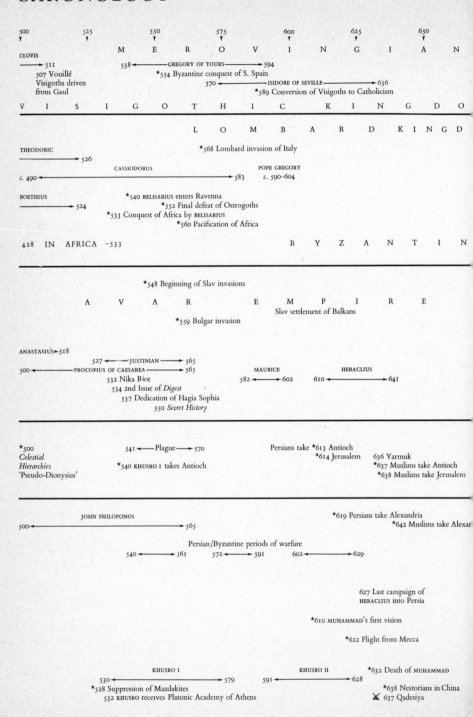

| 500 | 525 | 550 | 575 | 600 | 625 | 650 |

M E R O V I N G I A N

CLOVIS
→ 511
507 Vouillé
Visigoths driven
from Gaul

538 ←——— GREGORY OF TOURS ———→ 594
*554 Byzantine conquest of S. Spain
570 ←——— ISIDORE OF SEVILLE ———→ 636
*589 Conversion of Visigoths to Catholicism

V I S I G O T H I C   K I N G D O

L O M B A R D   K I N G D

THEODORIC
———→ 526

*568 Lombard invasion of Italy

CASSIODORUS
c. 490 ←——————————————→ 583

POPE GREGORY
c. 590–604

BOETHIUS
———→ 524

*540 BELISARIUS enters Ravenna
*552 Final defeat of Ostrogoths
*533 Conquest of Africa by BELISARIUS
*560 Pacification of Africa

428   IN   AFRICA   −533

B Y Z A N T I N

*548 Beginning of Slav invasions

A V A R   E M P I R E

Slav settlement of Balkans

*559 Bulgar invasion

ANASTASIUS →518
527 ←——— JUSTINIAN ———→ 565
500 ←——— PROCOPIUS OF CAESAREA ———→ 565
532 Nika Riot
534 2nd Issue of *Digest*
537 Dedication of Hagia Sophia
550 *Secret History*

MAURICE
582 ←——→ 602

HERACLIUS
610 ←——————→ 641

*500
Celestial
Hierarchies
'Pseudo-Dionysius'

541 ←——— Plague ———→ 570
*540 KHUSRO I takes Antioch

Persians take *613 Antioch
*614 Jerusalem   636 Yarmuk
*637 Muslims take Antioch
*638 Muslims take Jerusalem

JOHN PHILOPONOS
500 ←——————————————→ 565

*619 Persians take Alexandria
*642 Muslims take Alexan

Persian/Byzantine periods of warfare
540 ←——→ 361   572 ←——→ 591   602 ←——————→ 629

627 Last campaign of
HERACLIUS into Persia

*610 MUHAMMAD's first vision

*622 Flight from Mecca

KHUSRO I
530 ←——————————————→ 579
*528 Suppression of Mazdakites
532 KHUSRO receives Platonic Academy of Athens

KHUSRO II
591 ←——————→ 628

*632 Death of MUHAMMAD

*638 Nestorians in China
✕ 637 Qadesiya

700	725	750	775	800	825

VENERABLE BEDE

←————————→ 735

*711 Muslims invade Spain

✗ 732 Poitiers: defeat of Muslims by Franks

*800 Coronation of
CHARLEMAGNE

SPAIN   507–711

*698 Muslims take Carthage

E   X   A   R   C   H   A   T   E

7 Muslim siege of Constantinople

680 Sixth Oecumenical Council

717 Defeat of Muslims at Constantinople

*706/14 Great Mosque at Damascus

*695 First Muslim coins minted

*699 Arab replaces Greek in administration

692 ←————————→ 724
AL-HAJJAJ governor of Mesopotamia

*750 Revolt of the Abbasids

UMAYYAD   CALIFATE   660–750

*762 Foundation
of Baghdad

HARUN AL-RASHID
788 ←————→ 809

BIBLIOGRAPHY

For the reasons I have given, this book cannot be merely a history of the Decline and Fall of the Roman Empire. This problem has produced many an acute analysis of the economic and political weaknesses of the Roman state: see, recently, F.W. WALBANK, *The Awful Revolution* (Liverpool 1969) and the survey of learned opinion by S. MAZZARINO, *The End of the Ancient World* (London 1966). Nor is this book a survey of administrative and social structures, for which A.H.M. JONES, *The Later Roman Empire*, 3 vols (Oxford 1964) – referred to as JONES, *LRE* – is fundamental. The changing relations of groups within the Roman world and the interplay of their divergent cultural traditions concerns me directly – on which subject, R. MACMULLEN, *Soldier and Civilian in the Later Roman Empire* (Cambridge, Mass. 1963) and *Enemies of the Roman Order* (Oxford 1967) contain much of value. I have attempted to justify, at length, many of the interpretations advanced in this survey, in articles now collected as *Religion and Society in the Age of Saint Augustine* (London 1971).

CHAPTER I. M. ROSTOVTZEFF, *Social and Economic History of the Roman Empire*, 2 vols (2nd ed. Oxford 1957) is basic, with F. MILLAR et al., *The Roman Empire and its Neighbours* (London 1967). G. BOWERSOCK, *Greek Sophists in the Roman Empire* (Oxford 1969) and F. MILLAR, *A Study of Cassius Dio* (Oxford 1964) are outstanding studies.

CHAPTER II. The changes in the third century can no longer be regarded as the end of ancient civilization (as by Rostovtzeff, *op. cit.*): the extent of their impact has been more strictly delimited by R. RÉMONDON, *La crise de l'empire romain* (Paris 1964) and MILLAR, *The Roman Empire*.

On the formation of a new governing class and its repercussions on religion and culture, see A.H.M. JONES, 'The Social Background of the Struggle between Paganism and Christianity', *The Conflict between Paganism and Christianity*, ed. Momigliano (Oxford 1963). On late Roman upper-class culture: H.I. MARROU, *History of Education in the Ancient World* (London 1956) and *Saint Augustin et la fin de la culture antique* (4th ed. Paris 1958). Scholars in politics: A. CAMERON, 'Wandering Poets: a literary movement in Byzantine Egypt', *Historia* XIV (1965).

CHAPTER III. A. PIGANIOL, *L'Empire chrétien*, Histoire romaine IV, 2 (Paris 1947) is the best survey of the fourth century. For the new 'style' in political and social life: S. MAZZARINO, *Aspetti sociali del quarto secolo* (Rome 1951); L. HARMAND, *Le Patronat* (Paris 1957); and, on a revealing detail, G. DE STE-CROIX, 'Suffragium: from Vote to Patronage', *British Journal of Sociology* V (1954). On the more theatrical style of public deportment and ceremonial, and its popular origins: R. MACMULLEN, 'Some Pictures in Ammianus Marcellinus', *Art Bulletin* XLVI (1964). Local aristocracies: K. STROHEKER, *Der senatorische Adel im spätantiken Gallien* (Tübingen 1948) and A. CHASTAGNOL, *La préfecture urbaine à Rome sous le Bas-Empire* (Paris 1960). Towns and palaces: R. MEIGGS, *Roman Ostia* (Oxford 1960) and D. LEVI, *Antioch Mosaic Pavements* (Princeton 1947). The economic contrast of East and West: JONES, *LRE*, II, 1064–68. On the strength of urban life in the East, see P. PETIT, *Libanius et la vie municipale à Antioche* (Paris 1955) and D. CLAUDE, *Die byzantinische Stadt im VI. Jht.* (Munich 1969). The deep roots of the imperial autocracy in the East have been stressed by F. DVORNIK, *Early Christian and Byzantine Political Philosophy* (Washington 1966).

CHAPTER IV. A.-J. FESTUGIÈRE, *La Révélation d'Hermès Trismégiste*, 4 vols (Paris 1944–54) and E.R. DODDS, *Pagan and Christian in an Age of Anxiety* (Cambridge 1965) are brilliant characterizations of the change in religious sentiment. Despite random speculation, as in *Le Origini dello Gnosticismo*, Studies in the History of Religions, XII (Leiden 1967), we know little about the social background of these changes – see P. BROWN, 'Approaches to the Religious Crisis of the Third Century', *English Historical Review* LXXXIII (1968).

CHAPTER V. A.D. NOCK, *Conversion* (Oxford 1933) describes the spread and social significance of new cults in the Roman empire. Yet a study of the social context of Christianity is lacking. A. HARNACK, *The Mission and Expansion of Christianity* (London 1904/5, revised 1908) analyzes the evidence, taken largely from Eusebius, *The History of the Church* (Penguin Classics: London 1965). W.H.C. FREND, *Martyrdom and Persecution in the Early Church* (Oxford 1965) is thought-provoking, if partial. We know far more about the opposition of pagan society to the Christian Church (and vice versa!): see ORIGEN, *Contra Celsum*, transl. H. Chadwick

210

(2nd ed. Cambridge 1967), for pagan criticisms, and G. DE STE-CROIX, 'Why were the Early Christians persecuted?', *Past and Present* XXVI (1963).

CHAPTER VI. F. MILLAR, 'Dexippus', *Journal of Roman Studies* LIX (1969) has demonstrated the tenacity of the Greek aristocracies and intelligentsia, that forms a background to the Neoplatonic revival. On Plotinus, E. R. DODDS, 'Tradition and Personal Achievement in the Philosophy of Plotinus', *Journal of Roman Studies* L (1960) and P. HADOT, *Plotin* (Paris 1963) are the surest guides. For the later Platonists, see *The Cambridge History of Later Greek and Early Medieval Philosophy*, ed. A. Armstrong (Cambridge 1967). On Neoplatonism in the West, P. BROWN, *Augustine of Hippo* (London 1967); in Alexandria, J. MARROU, 'Synesius of Cyrene', *The Conflict between Paganism and Christianity*; in Athens, A. CAMERON, 'The Last Days of the Academy at Athens', *Proceedings of the Cambridge Philological Society* CXLV (1969). On the pervasive influence of Late Antique paganism on the world-view of the Middle Ages, see C. S. LEWIS, *The Discarded Image* (Cambridge 1964).

CHAPTER VII. On Constantine: A. H. M. JONES, *Constantine and the Conversion of Europe* (London 1948). Yet, compared with the attention lavished on the religious statecraft of Constantine, the intellectual climate of the age is less well known: see J. GEFFCKEN, *Der Ausgang des griechisch-römischen Heidentums* (Heidelberg 1920) and A. PIGANIOL, *L'Empereur Constantin* (Paris 1932). On the growth of the autocracy under Constantius II, see G. DAGRON, 'L'Empire romain d'Orient au IV siècle et les traditions politiques de l'hellénisme', *Travaux et mémoires* III (1968). On Julian, J. BIDEZ, *Vie de l'empereur Julien* (Paris, reprint 1965) and his *Works* (transl. Wright, Loeb Classical Library, 3 vols, 1953–54) – we need a new study! Christianity and classical culture: N. H. BAYNES, 'Hellenistic Civilisation and East Rome', *Byzantine Studies and Other Essays* (London 1955) and M. L. W. LAISTNER, *Christianity and Pagan Culture in the Later Roman Empire* (Cornell 1951) – and local culture, P. BROWN, 'Christianity and Local Culture in Late Roman North Africa', *Journal of Roman Studies* LVIII (1968).

CHAPTER VIII. D. CHITTY, *The Desert a City* (Oxford 1966) is humane and reliable. A. VÖÖBUS, *A History of Asceticism in the Syrian Orient*, II (Louvain 1960), is a spectacular portrait of Syrian eccentricity. The role of the saint in Byzantine society is best illustrated through the translations made available in E. DAWES and N. H. BAYNES, *Three Byzantine Saints* (Oxford 1948) and A.-J. FESTUGIÈRE, *Les Moines d'Orient*, 4 vols (Paris 1961–65). On almsgiving and the wealth of the Church: JONES, *LRE*, II, 920–29 and 970 ff. F. VAN DER MEER, *Early Christian Art* (transl. Peter and Friedl Brown, London 1967) is excellent on the style and function of ecclesiastical art.

CHAPTER IX. S. DILL, *Roman Society in the Last Century of the Western Empire* (London 1898: Meridian 1958) remains a delightful and comprehensive guide. On aristocratic paganism: H. BLOCH, 'The Pagan Revival in the West', *The Conflict between Paganism and Christianity*, modified by P. Brown 'Aspects of the Christianisation of the Roman Aristocracy', *Journal of Roman Studies* LI (1961) and A. CAMERON, 'The Date and Identity of Macrobius' *Journal of Roman Studies* LVI (1966). Latin culture: P. COURCELLE, *Les lettres grecques en Occident* (Paris 1948), now transl. H. E. WADECK, *Late Latin Writers and their Greek Sources* (Cambridge, Mass. 1969); P. CAMUS, *Ammien Marcellin* (Paris 1967); R. SYME, *Ammianus and the Historia Augusta* (Oxford 1968); P. BROWN, 'Pelagius and his Supporters', and 'The Patrons of Pelagius', *Journal of Theological Studies*, n.s. XIX (1968) and XXI (1970). ALAN CAMERON, *Claudian* (Oxford 1970). No study has yet found the measure of the culture and idiosyncrasy of Jerome. For the social and political attitudes of the aristocracy: F. PASCHOUD, *Roma aeterna* (Paris 1966).

Outstanding studies of the structure of the barbarian tribes and of their adaptation of Roman conditions are by E. A. THOMPSON, *The Early Germans* (Oxford 1965), *The Visigoths in the Time of Ulfilas* (Oxford 1966), *The Goths in Spain* (Oxford 1969). Against many scholars who stress the imperceptible evolution of a sub-Roman 'barbarian' society in the West, I would stress the self-conscious intolerance of the Roman population as a factor in 'encapsulating' the barbarian minorities: see P. COURCELLE, *Histoire littéraire des grandes invasions germaniques* (Paris 1964) and M. WALLACE-HADRILL, 'Gothia and Romania', *The Long-Haired Kings* (London 1962). The Franks, who were 'integrated', enjoyed a notably different fortune as a Catholic governing class, as Wallace-Hadrill, *op. cit.*, rightly insists.

CHAPTER X. In general: M. WALLACE-HADRILL, *The Barbarian West* (Oxford 1966). Sidonius Apollinaris is his own best expositor: see *The Letters of Sidonius*, transl. O.M. Dalton (Oxford 1915) and C.E. STEVENS, *Sidonius Apollinaris* (Oxford 1961). Gregory of Tours's *History of the Franks* is translated by O.M. Dalton (Oxford 1927): see WALLACE-HADRILL, 'The Work of Gregory of Tours', *The Long-Haired Kings*. For Italy, A. MOMIGLIANO, 'Cassiodorus and the Italian Culture of his Time', *Proceedings of the British Academy* XLI (1955) and M. WES, *Das Ende des Kaisertums im Westen des römischen Reichs* (The Hague 1967), are excellent. The survey of J. RICHÉ, *Education et Culture dans l'Occident barbare* (Paris 1962) has the merit of emphasizing the social function of classical culture in the West. Justinian's Reconquest was viewed with misgivings by many contemporaries (see Chapter XII), and, today, by those western medievalists who tend to regard the papacy as an essentially 'western' institution and Rome as a capital of the 'West', and so dismiss the eastern emperors as regrettable interlopers: P. LLEWELLYN, *Rome in the Dark Ages* (London 1971) provides evidence to correct this opinion.

CHAPTER XI. The social and economic history of the eastern empire: JONES, *LRE*, I, 202–37. On Constantinople: H.G. BECK, 'Senat und Volk von Konstantinopel', *Bayerische Akademie der Wissenschaften* (1966) and G. DOWNEY, *Constantinople in the Age of Justinian* (London 1964). Hippodrome and Circus-factions: A. CAMERON, *Porphyrius the Charioteer* (Oxford 1971). Latin and the idea of empire in Constantinople: G. DAGRON, 'Aux origines de la civilisation byzantine: langue de culture et langue d'Etat', *Revue Historique* CCXLI (1969). G. MATHEW, *Byzantine Aesthetics* (London 1963) is a brilliant evocation of tastes and outlook of the scholar-bureaucrats.

The prosperity and creativity of the eastern provinces: P. DU BOURGUET, *L'Art Copte* (Paris 1968); G. TCHALENKO, *Villages antiques de la Syrie du Nord*, 3 vols (Paris 1953–58) and J.B. SEGAL, *Edessa. The Blessed City* (Oxford 1970). Byzantine piety depended on these provinces: P. PEETERS, *Le tréfonds oriental de l'hagiographie byzantine* (Brussels 1950) and G. MATHEW, 'The Christian Background', *The Cambridge Medieval History* IV, I (Cambridge 1966). Hence the bitter opposition to the rise of Constantinople as an ecclesiastical 'capital' of the empire: N.H. BAYNES, 'Alex-

andria and Constantinople', *Byzantine Studies*. Study of the repercussions of the Council of Chalcedon has been obscured less by theological prejudice than by the determination of most modern scholars to explain – or to explain away! – the religious opposition of eastern provincials as an expression of social or political discontent: A.H.M. JONES, 'Were the Ancient Heresies national or social movements in disguise?', *Journal of Theological Studies*, n.s. X (1959), provides a corrective and *Das Konzil von Chalkedon*, ed. A. GRILLMEIR and H. BACHT, 2 vols (Würzburg 1951–53) enough material for the alert reader to make up his mind. On Anastasius: P. CHARANIS, *Church and State in the Later Roman Empire* (Madison 1939).

CHAPTER XII. P.N. URE. *Justinian and His Age* (Pelican, Harmondsworth 1951) is written with zest. The black picture of Procopius, in his *Secret History* (transl. G.A. Williamson, Penguin Classics, Harmondsworth 1969), and implied in much of the *History of the Wars* (transl. by Dewing, Loeb Classical Library, London and New York 1914–40) still influences modern views. JONES, *LRE*, I, pp. 266–302, is the fairest account.

On military problems: J. TEALL, 'Barbarians in the Armies of Justinian', *Speculum* XL (1965). On the development of Byzantine diplomacy: D. OBOLENSKY, 'The Empire and its Northern Neighbours', *The Cambridge Medieval History* IV, I (Cambridge 1966) – a masterly survey (also includes a discussion of the Slav settlements).

CHAPTER XIII. Persia proper: A. CHRISTENSEN, *L'Iran sous les Sassanides* (Copenhagen-Paris 1936) and R. FRYE, *The Heritage of Persia* (London 1963). *Persia e il mondo grecoromano* (Rome 1966) contains some relevant essays.

On the social and religious life of Mesopotamia: B. SEGAL, 'The Mesopotamian communities from Julian to the Rise of Islam', *Proceedings of the British Academy* XLI (1955), J. NEUSNER, *A History of the Jews in Babylonia*, vols II–V (Leiden 1966–70) and V. PIGULEVSKAJA, *Les villes dans l'état iranien* (Paris 1963). Cultural relations with Byzantium through the Mesopotamian Christian communities: P. BROWN, 'The Diffusion of Manichaeism in the Roman Empire', *Journal of Roman Studies* LIX (1969). Byzantine attitudes to Persia: AVERIL CAMERON, 'Agathias on the Sassanians', *Dumbarton Oaks Papers* XXIII (1969).

CHAPTER XIV. Many historians treat the reign of Justinian as the tragic climax of the late Roman state, and pass on to the reign of Heraclius as the beginning of medieval Byzantium. As a result, the late sixth century has been neglected as a period of crucial interest in its own right. The classical tradition in the late sixth century: AVERIL CAMERON, 'The "Scepticism" of Procopius', *Historia* xv (1966) and *Agathias* (Oxford 1970). John Philoponos: S. SAMBURSKY, *The Physical World of Late Antiquity* (London 1962). The preservation of classical texts: L. REYNOLDS and N. WILSON, *Scribes and Scholars* (Oxford 1968). For western Europe: J. FONTAINE, *Isidore de Séville et la culture classique de l'Espagne Wisigothique*, 2 vols (Paris 1959). Popular religious culture: E. KITZINGER, 'The Cult of Images in the Age before Iconoclasm', *Dumbarton Oaks Papers* VIII (1954).

CHAPTER XV. TOR ANDRAE, *Mohammed* (London 1936), stresses the sources of Muhammad's teaching in Near Eastern ascetic piety, and M. WATT, *Muhammed at Mecca* and *Muhammad at Medina* (Oxford 1953 and 1955) the immediate problems of Arab society. I. GOLDZIHER, *Muslim Studies*, transl. S. Stern (London 1968) sees clearly the tension between what Islam preached and what the Beduin were prepared to practise.

CHAPTER XVI. V. MONNERET DE VILLARD, *Introduzione allo studio dell'archaeologia islamica* (Venice 1966), is a brilliant account of the continuity of social and artistic forms in the Near East. For the survival of Late Antique culture, Byzantine and Persian, and their reception by the Arabs: GOLDZIHER, *op. cit.*; R. WALZER, *Greek into Arabic* (London 1962), and R. PARET, 'Contribution à l'étude des milieux culturels dans le Proche-Orient médiévale', *Revue Historique* CCXXXV (1966). A shift of the centre of gravity of wealth and civilization away from the Mediterranean coast, in the rise of the Abbasid califate (on which now see *Islam and the Trade of Asia*, ed. D. S. Richards (London 1971) may explain the change in the development of commerce and culture in western Europe that so preoccupied H. PIRENNE, *Mahomet and Charlemagne* (transl. Miall, London 1937). Pirenne's thesis is still hotly, and fruitfully, debated: see A. RIISING, 'The Fate of H. Pirenne's thesis on the consequences of the Islamic Expansion', *Classica et Medievalia* XIII (1952).

ACKNOWLEDGMENTS

Albi, Bibliothèque Municipale: 4. Antioch, Museum of Antiquities: 33. Aquileia, Archaeological Museum: 55. Archives Photographiques: 7, 65. Athens, National Archaeological Museum: 56. Bardo Museum, Tunisia: 28, 29, 34. Bargello, Florence: 89, 92. Beny, Roloff: 3. Biblioteca Ambrosiana, Milan: 51. Biblioteca Apostolica Vaticana: 50, 58, 59, 85, 115. Biblioteca Medicea-Laurenziana, Florence: 124. Bibliothèque Nationale, Paris: 104, 106, 113, 119. Bildarchiv Marburg: 99. Brescia, Museo Civico: 1, 83. British Museum, London: 15, 22, 60, 101, 109, 114, 121. Capitoline Museum, Rome: 53. Christie's, London: 70. Clayton, Peter: 121. Deutsches Archaeologisches Institut, Rome: 6, 10, 13, 26, 42. Dayton, J.E.: 129, 130. Dumbarton Oaks Collection, Washington, D.C.: 57, 68, 77. Editions Gallimard: 11, 25, 44, 46, 47, 75, 76, 95, 97, 106, 107, 110, 116, 117. Gabinetto Nazionale Fotografico, Rome: 26, 27, 36, 41, 82. Halle, Landesmuseum: 80. Hermitage, Leningrad: 31, 120. Hirmer Fotoarchiv: 32, 62, 63, 88, 93, 98, 100, 104, 111, 112, 123, 125. Istanbul, Archaeological Museum: 35, 93, 125. Kunsthistorisches Museum, Vienna: 24, 29. Louvre, Paris: 7, 65, 69, 72. Madrid, Archaeological Museum: 122. Madrid, Academia de la Historia: 75. Mansell Collection (Alinari): 30, 38, 45, 53, 54, 66, 74, 78, 79, 88, 90, 102, 103. Mas: 81, 86. Masson, Georgina, Rome: 61. Metropolitan Museum of Art, New York: 128. Monza, Cathedral Treasury: 87, 117. Ostia, Museum: 23. Osterreichische Nationalbibliothek, Vienna: 105, 126, 127. Pushkin Museum, Moscow: 73. Recklinghausen, Ikonenmuseum: 8. Rossano, Cathedral Treasury: 32. Scala: 2, 12. Schweizerisches Landesmuseum, Zürich: 98. Staatliche Museen, Berlin: 37, 62, 67, 94, 96, 108. Speyer, Historisches Museum: 9. Teheran, Archaeological Museum: 110. Trier, Cathedral Treasury: 99. Vatican Museums: 5, 40, 48, 52, 54, 115. Vick (Barcelona), Episcopal Museum: 86. Victoria and Albert Museum, London: 21, 39. Yale University Art Gallery: 43.

INDEX